NGOs
and
Human Rights

NGOs AND HUMAN RIGHTS

By

Dr. M. Lakshmi Narasaiah
M.A., Ph.D.

Professor of Economics,
Co-ordinator, Department of M.B.A. and Commerce,
Special Officer,
Sri Krishnadevaraya University Post-graduate Centre,
Kurnool–518 002
Andhra Pradesh (India)

DISCOVERY PUBLISHING HOUSE
NEW DELHI

First Published-2006

Reprint : 2012

ISBN 81-8356-061-X

Published by

DISCOVERY PUBLISHING HOUSE

4831/24, Ansari Road, Prahlad Street,
Darya Ganj, New Delhi-110002 (India)
Phone: 23279245 • Fax: 91-11-23253475
E-mail:dphtemp@indiatimes.com

Printed at

Dynamic Printers,

Preface

A moment is needed to take stock and to look at the deficits, which still exist in terms of human rights half a century later. The Declaration of 1948 contains a comprehensive list of political, economic, social and cultural rights and aims at the protection of the freedom, equality, and human dignity of all human beings, irrespective of their race, gender, language or religion. Never before in history had there been such a far-reaching and solemn undertaking to protect each and every individual from all forms of oppression and deprivation. Two treaties adopted by the UN General Assembly in 1966 translate the ideas of the Human Rights Declaration into binding international law, and a High Commissioner for Human Rights, an office created as a result of the UN Human Rights Conference in Vienna in 1993, has been put in charge of monitoring the human rights situation and coordinate UN action on it. Numerous human rights NGOs all over the world, most important among them Amnesty International, have established themselves as additional watchdogs to guard against human rights violations.

But in spite of all the attention, human rights issues are receiving, especially in the Western democracies, the progress achieved in guaranteeing fundamental human rights to every individual is anything but satisfactory. It is true with the collapse of fascism and communism, and the disappearance of many of the military regimes in Latin America, Asia and Africa, some of the ugliest tyrants who trampled human rights under their feet have gone. Democratic structures are on the advance, and with them a certain measure of rule of law. In more and more countries, governments are elected by the people which means that they are to some extent accountable to their voters and cannot violate human rights with impunity. However, even where there is formal democracy and elections are periodically being held, social-economic or cultural rights are persistently denied to large groups of people.

In Africa millions of girls are circumcised (female genital mutilation) with grave consequences for their physical and psychological well-being—a serious violation of their human rights although defended by African males as cultural practice. In India, "the world's largest democracy", millions of dalits suffer from discrimination and exclusion because they do not belong to the caste system. Tens of millions of children are forced to work under harsh conditions, ruining their health and missing opportunities for education; bonded labours are toiling for rich landowners in rural areas; and girls and women are suppressed by customs which still grant all the economic power to men. There are good laws in India, which forbid all these practices, but the laws are not enforced in the absence of strong institutions which reach down to the village level.

This is the situation in many countries: the existing legal framework guarantees the protection of human rights as enshrined in the UN Declaration. But the reality is quite different.

All these are accounts of the daily violations of human rights which are going on in many countries and which throw a long and dark shadow over the human rights. Most of those oppressed and stripped of their rights are poor people, those on the lowest range of the scale. Because they are poor, they find it almost impossible to assert their rights, which they may hold under the constitution and the laws of the country in which they live. They are often illiterate and do not even know their rights, and when they do, they have no money to pay a lawyer and to go to court: For many of the more than 1 billion people living in abject poverty, human rights therefore do not exist in reality. They are far from being able to live a life in dignity as demanded by the UN Declaration.

Human rights, therefore, cannot be protected in isolation from economic and social factors. If we manage to reduce poverty, we will also help to improve the human rights situation. Development policy thus becomes a key to the problem without the enforcement of political human rights, social human rights cannot permanently be secured. On the other hand, the realisation of political human rights depends to a large extent on favourable economic, social and cultural conditions.

Human rights, when denied to people, can be a source of internal or external conflict—just think of the millions of refugees who had to leave their homes due to ethnic and religious strife. The world would therefore be a safer place if full human rights were granted to all individuals in the world as proclaimed in the UN Declaration fifty years ago. Peace and progress would be the reward if we achieve this noble goal.

Dr. M. Lakshmi Narasaiah

Contents

1

NGOs: *Searching for Solid Ground*

The role of NGOs should be to foster the emergence of a world wide civil society, the first step towards making globalisation a more democratic affair. NGOs were not born yesterday, but the rising number of conflicts that have reverberated in recent decades around a world globalized in the neoliberal mould has led them to multiply and diversify into highly visible bodies.

Who are the main players in this process of globalisation? Governments (politics) and the market (the economy) are the twin pillars supporting the productive systems and structures of modern societies. So who has the legitimate right to change them? The societies themselves, for they alone are made up of citizens grouped together as a people, a nation or a country. The right does not belong to governments, state structures, corporate executives or markets. This is why, as NGOs, our attention is directed at civil society itself.

At the global level, our basic task is to foster the emergence of a worlwide civil society as a precondition to calling for a new style of globalisation: "world governance." Our mission is to encourage the refounding of globalisation along more democratic lines by taking part in public debate and promulgating the concept of world citizenship. The political stances we take and our lobbying activities, therefore, do not come out of the blue but are efforts to transmit the main currents and aspirations of public opinion and make this opinion stronger and clearer.

The Tripartite Mirage

All NGO actions are based on an obvious priority, namely that of supporting social protests and public pressure during major negotiations taking place within the main circles of power. That is why the agreements we conclude and the alliances we forge are above all else aimed at organisations and movements arising from civil society. That is also why we build forums, coalitions and networks that straddle national borders. On the basis of our approach, we can think globally, set up links between the particular and the universal, swap experiences and keep ourselves regularly informed.

Today, global power is monopolized by major multilateral organisations, and is fundamentally anti-democratic in its structure and workings. In their current form, these organisations' claims to embody democracy and universal citizenship ring hollow. In fact, their only possible claim to legitimacy is through the vote. But not all the national governments represented in international organisations have been elected by popular suffrage, and very few of them represent all the different social forces that go into making up their nations.

Does this mean that NGOs, which are supposed to embody civil society, should claim to represent these peoples? Does it mean that our goal should be to win a place at the heart of a future new world democratic order? Does it mean that we are fully entitled to a seat in some new tripartite structure—made up of government, companies and civil society—that some people are campaigning for? In my opinion, all of that is just a mirage; even worse, we risk losing sight of our most useful and most legitimate purpose if we embrace that vision.

Small Players, Big Issues

NGOs are not out to conquer power or win elections, be they world, national or local bodies. We are not set up like political parties, even though our activities are public and seem highly politicized. We cannot even present ourselves as representatives of civil society because civil society has not entrusted us with any such mandate.

So what do we want? To reach out, mobilize, educate, get across messages, suggest, innovate, persuade and politically strengthen various groups in civil society and, more specifically, those excluded from the decision-making process. We want to give a voice to ideas, values, questions and proposals that involve social justice, a more equitable distribution of wealth, respect for the environment, the struggle against poverty and social exclusion.

Who are we? Small players, compared to the other pillars of civil society, such as trade unions and professional organisations, or bodies in the state or the market. But we are also—and this is something new—"big" players, because our mission and our field of action are not limited to a given society, national economy or single government. Our task is to form a bridge between the local and the global: in other words, to deal with what is universal, with what is common to all humanity. Human rights, social crises and environmental protection are global issues. We deal with them in specific situations, but our perspective is always planetary.

So where does our legitimacy lie? In the quality of the values, principles and ideals we defend. In the relevance and the importance of the issues we raise. In the inventiveness of the proposals we put forward. Our only source of legitimacy is our ability to develop ideas aimed at action—ideas that are up to the standards of public duty to which we aspire.

2

NGOs Better Than the State

Non-governmental organisations have become the new hope of development cooperation. Criticism of official and multilateral development assistance is mounting. After more than four decades of international cooperation, there is more poverty in the Third World (with the exception of a few countries) than ever before. It has become clear that existing instruments cannot bring about change. Even the large donor organisations doubt their own ability to solve problems and find their doubts confirmed by internal evaluations. What led to this state of affairs, and is there reason to hope that the NGOs can do a better job?

Development assistance started in 1949 with U.S. President Harry Truman's famous Point Four Programme (named after Point 4 of his inaugural speech in Congress on January 20, 1949) as a continuation of the Marshall Plan. The policy of containment of communism, which was originally restricted to Europe, thus became a global strategy. This origin was the reason that development assistance was geared from the beginning exclusively to governments, and not to social groups in the developing countries. The accusation that the U.S.A. as well as the other Western donors were willing to provide development assistance to any government, even the most under democratic and corrupt one, as long as it was an ally against communism, was never dropped.

Four decades later, when hardly anyone remembered the origins of this policy, the original goal was reached:

Communism collapsed. In the interim, development assistance became independent: what was merely a means to an end for Truman in 1949 had become the goal itself: Liberation of all people not only from oppression, but also from hunger, want and desperation. However, it was now conceded, although hesitantly, that this particular goal had not been met: that in many countries a corrupt and dictatorial state class had been kept alive rather than development, and that democratisation had in fact been obstructed.

Simultaneously, an intensive discussion of two new themes began in intellectual circles in the U.S. The return of ethics in politics and a stronger influence of citizens in public affairs—against the background of governments which were no longer trusted to be able to solve social problems. Both themes have by now reached. Europe under the labels "Communitarianism" and "civil society" where they were taken up by the "new social movements." These include North-NGOs which are active in development cooperation and work with partner organisations in the south. It is important not to lose sight of this correlation with society's broader change of values.

The NGOs argue that they can circumvent the unwieldy bureaucratic planning and administration process; that they are flexible, efficient, close to the target groups, and democratic at the grassroots level, and that their funds flow directly to the poor. How accurate is this claim?

Little is known in the North about the NGOs of the South. The rural reconstruction movements, which exist in several Asian countries, date back to the twenties. Today, they are large organisations with hundreds or thousand of staff members. In India and Sri Lanka, groups try to realize the ideas of Mahatama Gandhi. In Africa, self-help and solidarity groups at the village level have been a tradition for centuries. Ethnologists used to characterize them as "secret societies". The large organisations, which were established in Africa (later than in Asia) a few years ago, build on this tradition. In Latin America, an attempt is made to revive the models of cooperative work in the pre-Columbian era.

It is a myth that these groups are egalitarian grassroots organisations. Those that actually function, at the village as well as at the regional or national level, do so thanks to the selfless involvement of individual persons, who are able to motivate others, come up with ideas, coordinate efforts, and bring about decisions. Social science has known since the studies of group dynamics and "democratic leadership" in the U.S. in the thirties that groups cannot be effective without such people. In the North they cannot work "directly with the poor" because this would presuppose that again we would be on location. The assistance depends on the cooperation of local organisations, which means their leaders. We tend to forget this too easily in our development jargon. The real chance for NGO leaders lies in the fact that they do not have to prevail against a rigid, bureaucratic apparatus, which tries to stop novel ideas just because they are new. On the other hand, this constellation also harbours the danger that imperiousness and autocratic structures will expand within the NGO sector just as at the state level. Who actually monitors the NGOs? Not just government ministers have been known to build their own private residences with development aid money. Some NGO executives are already guilty of doing the same.

3

No Miracle Weapon for Development

The Challenges Facing NGOs in the 21st Century

Not only official development policy, but also the work of NGOs has come under pressure to reform. The optimistic belief that cooperation with NGO partners in the South would lead quasi automatically to better results has faded. In this sector, too, questions are being asked about efficiency control, better coordination, and focus instead of a 'shotgun' approach to the work.

In the case of NGOs engaged in development policy, it is not only their standing that has become greater. Their number, budgets and influence—and their closeness to governments—have also gained in quantity and strength. NGOs are now 'in' with governments, the media and international development cooperation agencies. NGOs are seen as the 'miracle weapon' in the battle against increasing poverty in large parts of the world.

The NGOs closeness to grassroots organisations in the South, their emphasis on help for self-help, and their independence from the foreign policy and economic interests of the North, allows them to orient their cooperation activities on the basic needs of the people in developing countries. And that enables the NGOs to make a credible and effective contribution to social change. But this self-made claim leads the public to expect big things of the organisations, which perhaps cannot be fulfilled.

The NGOs have largely failed to address this point, thereby missing the opportunity to take a self-critical look at themselves. Only such a stock taking, however, would permit answers to the question of what the NGOs will stand for in the 21st century.

To claim that we could give the answer in this article would be presumptuous. But we would like to outline three challenges which, we believe, the NGOs should in future tackle more robustly. In doing so, we shall concentrate on North NGOs and their branches in the developing countries.

Focus on Core Tasks

NGOs are increasingly assuming tasks, which earlier were the domain of government actors. For example, the organisations support, among the things, the expansion of infrastructure in urban as well as rural areas, and public health and education systems. Various factors are helping to drive this development.

First, the neo-liberal concepts of many structural adjustment programmes have made developing country governments pull out of political areas which in most industrialised nations are controlled by governments, if not implemented by them.

Second, donor governments are happy to give up cooperating with inefficient and sometimes intractable official partner structures if NGOs offer themselves as competent intermediaries or implementing organisations.

Third, the industrialised nations' development cooperation agencies score a double coup by such switching of responsibility for a project. They gain vicarious kudos from the NGO's positive image, and moreover can be pretty sure that the NGO side will not criticise the measures.

Finally, in line with the liberal ethos on democracy, the NGOs are regarded as the champions of democratisation and the foundation of a civil society.

This leads to the NGOs running the risk of obligingly allowing themselves to be instrumentalised as the fill-in for the cut backs and failures of official development cooperation and becoming the victims of their own claims. To date, nothing has indicated that, measured against developmental benchmarks such as effectiveness, efficiency and significance, the quality of NGO inputs in such sectors as infrastructure and advisory services for parastatals is better than that of government implementation organisations.

An undisputed strength of the North NGOs is that they have good contacts with their local counterparts of self-help initiatives, and many years' experience in this sector. But being close to the grassroots reduces the financial volume of potential intervention because that depends to a great degree on the limited capacity of the partner on site to absorb large sums of money. Moreover, North NGOs are as a rule too small and too diversified to achieve the degree of specialisation necessary for professional assessment and supervision of promotional measures. Not least, the NGO's target groups want mostly a package of measures more akin to community development approaches than to single sector projects.

These strengths and weaknesses present guidelines for defining the NGOs' core tasks. They should focus on their strengths to give their profile sharper edges. That includes pointing out to the industrialised nations development cooperation agencies their own core missions. Instead of perfoming in non-government sectors, to which its instruments are not suited, official development cooperation should, rather, ensure that developing country governments and their administrative bodies can competently fulfil their tasks.

Cooperation Instead of Competition

Whoever travels through developing countries today, sees at many crossroads signs that point in all directions to the locations of local NGOs. Not all NGOs are competent, not all are grassroots-oriented, and not a few are simply labels for private business sector initiatives or the sinecures of representatives of the state elite. Neither representatives of North NGOs nor government implementing organisations find it easy to separate the wheat from the chaff. But in only a few (praiseworthy) cases is there an exchange of information among the international actors, apparently because every organisation wants to shield its local partners from the others.

This had led on the one hand to the South NGOs also having long played the game known in official development cooperation circles as 'donor rotation'. As soon as one donor completes a project, another steps into replace him. Interventions also are too often not harmonised.

This criticism does not mean there should be no competition to find the best solution to a problem. On the contrary, specific processes should be made transparent and discussed so that one can differentiate between reports of short-lived success and approaches aligned on the long haul. Indeed, perhaps that would enable learning from others and lead to good ideas being taken up by several. Many North NGOs appear not even to have a need for reciprocal information flows and case-to-case harmonisation, which are gradually gaining a foothold in official development cooperation—although with many setbacks due to well-known national interests.

So long as there is no government framework for their activities, NGOs should strengthen their attempts to harmonise their support measures with other actors. This does not contradict NGO enterprise. An unfortunately frequent deficit of developing countries is that their governments do not define scope for developmental action. This means that both official and non-governmental development cooperation operates in a political vacuum which gives every well-meaning dilettante room for experiments.

NGOs can be proud of their contribution to the consolidation of human rights in many societies, and of their efforts for civil rights and for more efficient local organisations with a greater capability to handle conflicts. NGOs also have won great credit by pointing out to government actors deficiencies and weak spots in developmental practice. Without the NGOs' pressure and that of their lobby, the cross-sectorial topics of the environment, women and poverty—which are now firmly fixed in development cooperation—would not have entered the international political debate so quickly nor have been implemented in projects and programmes.

NGOs would be well advised to get together as soon as possible to define and agree on criteria for the quality of their work. They should also carry out evaluations that identify and clearly describe the impacts of their efforts.

The basis of the evaluations should be a joint code or common denominator for the most important developmental benchmarks, such as sustainability and subsidiarity. This would be right for the peculiarities of the many NGOs, and not result in all organisations being lumped together.

Power or Importence Instrumentalised

NGOs are not the 'miracle weapon' they have allowed themselves to be labelled. Their positive image has so far been enough to retain the goodwill of members of the public who are interested in developmental matters, especially that of donors. But that can change quickly if the NGOs allow themselves to be instrumentalised by their own governments, if government organisations overtake them in efficiency control, and if they cannot convincingly present their core tasks for the present and future. That applies above all if they criticise others without putting their own house in order. And also if they aim to steal silently away from goals such as solidarity, social change and innovation.

It is not about random concepts, but central challenges. NGOs that want to do more than just survive but aim at effective, high-quality and professional work targeted on social change in partner countries should confront these challenges aggressively. Otherwise, the "Power of the Courageous" will one day turn into the importance of those who came too late.

4

Human Rights

The Road to Progress and Peace

The UN Declaration on Human Rights has been fifty years old. A moment is needed to take stock and to look at the deficits, which still exist in terms of human rights half a century later. The Declaration of 1948 contains a comprehensive list of political, economic, social and cultural rights and aims at the protection of the freedom, equality, and human dignity of all human beings, irrespective of their race, gender, language or religion. Never before in history had there been such a far-reaching and solemn undertaking to protect each and every individual from all forms of oppression and deprivation. Two treaties adopted by the UN General Assembly in 1966 translate the ideas of the Human Rights Declaration into binding international law, and a High Commissioner for Human Rights, an office created as a result of the UN Human Rights Conference in Vienna in 1993, has been put in charge of monitoring the human rights situation and coordinate UN action on it. Numerous human rights NGOs all over the world, most important among them Amnesty International, have established themselves as additional watchdogs to guard against human rights violations.

But in spite of all the attention, human rights issues are receiving, especially in the Western democracies, the progress achieved in guaranteeing fundamental human rights to every individual is anything but satisfactory. It is true with the collapse of fascism and communism, and the disappearance of many of the military regimes in Latin America, Asia and Africa, some of the ugliest tyrants who trampled human rights under their feet have gone. Democratic structures are on the advance, and with them a certain measure of rule of law. In more and more countries, governments are elected by the people which means that they are to some extent accountable to their voters and cannot violate human rights with impunity. However, even where there is formal democracy and elections are periodically being held, social-economic or cultural rights are persistently denied to large groups of people.

In Africa millions of girls are circumcised (female genital mutilation) with grave consequences for their physical and psychological well-being—a serious violation of their human rights although defended by African males as cultural practice. In India, "the world's largest democracy", millions of dalits suffer from discrimination and exclusion because they do not belong to the caste system. Tens of millions of children are forced to work under harsh conditions, ruining their health and missing opportunities for education; bonded labours are toiling for rich landowners in rural areas; and girls and women are suppressed by customs which still grant all the economic power to men. There are good laws in India, which forbid all these practices, but the laws are not enforced in the absence of strong institutions which reach down to the village level.

This is the situation in many countries: the existing legal framework guarantees the protection of human rights as enshrined in the UN Declaration. But the reality is quite different.

All these are accounts of the daily violations of human rights which are going on in many countries and which throw a long and dark shadow over the human rights. Most of those oppressed and stripped of their rights are poor people, those on the lowest range of the scale. Because they

One and a half billion people live in dire poverty—their most fundamental right. The right to life, the bedrock of all other rights, is constantly threatened. So the still unfinished struggle to extend and strengthen human rights includes the duty to promote development.

This duty is not only a matter of legal formalism or an ethical imperative. Fundamental freedoms will remain very fragile as long as poverty, exclusion and inequalities persist. The forces of globalisation encourage the establishment of the rule of law, but a version of law biased in favour of rules needed for successful business activity. They also do more to sharpen economic and social tensions rather than to reduce them.

The momentum created by efforts to establish the rule of law in a growing number of countries is coming up against a major obstacle. The principles and rules that govern international relations are increasing their influence on the lives of nations, but they are very far indeed from being democratic. The strongest still holds way.

This is true where individual states are concerned. They feel their wings have been clipped, and see their legitimate prerogatives being eroded by the rise of a kind of private-sector absolutism, which tends to limit the functions of government to security and mediation, paralysing its role as the guarantor of the general interest and depriving it of the necessary means to apply the rule of law.

It is also true of the community of states because there is still no world structure which is accepted as the embodiment of the force of law. The United Nations is a unique international democratic forum, but its authority has been weakened first by nearly half a century of the Cold War and then by unilateral actions taken by the major powers in defiance of the very principles they profess to defend. The rule of law is indivisible, it must encompass freedom and welfare, individual countries and the world at large.

6

Speaking from a Position of Economic Strength

The Human Rights Debate and Asia

The recent debate on "Asian Values" and human rights has developed into a cottage industry. At every turn politicians, academics and opportunists of all ilks are jumping on the bandwagon giving their version of what human rights are all about and whether Asia should be unique in its approach to human rights issues and its quest for democracy and modernity. Unfortunately, in issues of this kind, the debate attracts all sorts of people, each with their own specific agendas, and neither "Asian values" proponents nor opponents speak with one voice.

What is perhaps most surprising is how quickly the debate has polarised the camps, reviving the age-old divide between East and West. Taking a step back, however, is it really just cultural differences that separate the two camps? I think the real interests underpinning the debate have nothing at all to do with questions of culture, or indeed, even human rights. Rather, they are related to Asian economic success and confidence and Asia's continuing reaction to colonialism.

I doubt very much if this debate would have even started were late twentieth-century Asia nothing but a sea of poverty, degradation, and squalor. But it is not. Asia is booming, and economists and analysts alike are calling the next century the "Pacific Century" an obvious reference to the tremendous growth in the Asia-Pacific region. The Asian "economic miracle" has been linked to so-called Confucian and Asian values by no less venerable an institution than the World Bank. The linkage between economic growth and cultural values has given Asian leaders and intellectuals a newfound confidence in two ways. First, Asian voices, particularly those emanating from countries like Singapore, Malaysia, South Korea, Taiwan and Thailand, are standing up to their detractors with a confidence buoyed by their countries' double-digit growth. Second, economic success cloaks many of these Asian governments in what is called as "performance legitimacy." Countries in Asia are modernising and growing at an unprecedented pace, and Asian leaders and their people are justifiably proud of their achievements. The present Asian Financial crises is temporary.

In the face of such overwhelming success, new-found national pride pits Asian countries against the "decadent West", which constantly preaches to Asian nations to constantly preaches to Asian Nations to conform to what it believes to be universally established standards of human rights practice. Constant pressure to observe human rights obligations, often applied with threats of economic sanctions, is regarded by many as a slap in the Asian face and, more importantly, an attempt by the West to hold the East to ransom. Beyond a cursory flat denial of human rights violations, Asians must justify their actions, and one powerful way to do this is by claiming historical, cultural and religious exception. At the same time some Asian states push the cultural line to support their soft authoritarian form of governments, which have, together with their social and economic agendas, also come under attack from western leaders and intellectuals. In this sense, Asian states are really fighting for the right to be modern, not to forge their own version of human rights.

Most Asian scholars very keen on the "Asian values" debate because it is an opportunity to take on the West in an intellectual exchange where the West does not have a clear and distinct advantage.

The positions the West is taking in the debate are no different from those the West has always stood by. Media coverage in recent years, however, has impassioned the debate and has thus highlighted and, in some respects, shaped the divergence of interests between East and West. The stakes in the debate have come to be planted along civilizational lines that cut deep into the national and hemispheric pride of both parties. When the debate is couched in these terms, then all the other baggage is imported along with it. So I don't believe the West is overreacting in its response to the debate. I do, however, detect a sense of panic among many Western scholars and politicians—result of the fact that many Asians appear to be speaking from a position of strength; strength drawn not from the merits of intellectual arguments but from economic success.

Can the Western response be improved? It's difficult to say. The West is primarily concerned with the merits of the conceptual arguments. While the West is concerned with whether it is at all possible to take a relativist approach to human rights issues, Asia is more concerned with power politics. The East's reactions to this must, I think, be viewed in its proper context. The problem, as Asians see it, is this: How can the West, especially America, preach democracy and human rights as fundamental values when the West can't even get its own house in order? Asia, on the other hand, is less the hypocrite because it takes a culturally relativist approach to the situation and does not pretend to be the champion of human rights. Such is the view of many in Asia.

It is interesting to note that the human rights debate has without a doubt attracted more scholars, intellectuals, and politicians in the West than in Asia. There are two possible reasons for this. Western liberalism and its ideals are under threat, and this siege on the Western citadel has drawn more and more Western leaders and intellectuals into the fray, compelled to stage a spirited defense against Asia's confident and well-considered alternative world view. But, it could also be true that Asian intellectuals are just having too good a time enjoying their newly acquired wealth to worry so much about such conceptual debates.

7

Safe Motherhood is a Human Rights Issue

The death of a woman during pregnancy or childbirth is not only a health issue but also a matter of social injustice. Of the human rights currently acknowledged in national constitutions and in regional and international human rights treaties, many can be applied to safe motherhood. Many such treaties and conventions are based on the 1948 Declaration of Human Rights. They include (1); the Convention on the Elimination of All Forms of Discrimination against Women, (2), the Convention on the Rights of the Child, (3), the European Convention for the Protection of Human Rights and Fundamental Freedoms, (4), the American Convention on Human Rights, and (5), the African Charter on Human and Peoples' Rights (6).

Human rights of relevance to safe motherhood can be grouped into the following four principal categories:

- ***Rights relating to life, liberty and security of the person,*** which require governments to ensure both access to appropriate healthcare during pregnancy and childbirth, and women's rights to decide whether, when and how often to bear children. Governments must therefore address factors within the economic, legal, social and health systems that deny women these fundamental rights.

- ***Rights relating to the foundation of families and of family life,*** which require governments to provide access to health-services and other facilities that women need to establish families and to enjoy life within a family.

- ***Rights relating to healthcare and the benefits of scientific progress, including health information and education,*** which require governments to provide access to good sexual and reproductive healthcare with appropriate referral systems. The measures needed to ensure safe motherhood can be provided through primary healthcare irrespective of a country's level of economic development. Central to these rights is information on a range of reproductive health issues, including family planning, abortion and sex education.
- ***Rights relating to equality and non-discrimination,*** which require governments to provide access to services such as education and healthcare without discriminatory grounds such as sex, marital status, age and socio-economic class. Discriminatory policies include requirements for a woman to obtain the consent of her husband for particular healthcare interventions, requirements for parental authorisation which have a differential impact on girls, and laws that criminalise medical procedures that only women need. Governments are in violation of their obligations when they fail to implement laws that effectively protect women's interests or to allocate health resources to meet women's particular need for safe pregnancy and childbirth.

The actions that governments need to take to promote safe motherhood as a human right fall into three groups:

- ***Reform of laws*** that prevent women from attaining the highest possible levels of health and nutrition needed for safe pregnancy and childbirth and that inhibit access to reproductive health information and services such as laws requiring women in need of healthcare to seek the authorisation of husbands or other family members first.

- ***Implementation of laws*** that foster women's rights to good health and nutrition and that protect women's health interests such as laws that prohibit child marriage, female genital mutilation, rape and sexual abuse. Every effort should be made to implement laws that encourage the healthy timing of births, such as those that support the education of girls, set a minimum age for marriage and ensure women's access to essential healthcare.

- ***Application of human rights*** in national legislation and policy to advance safe motherhood.

8

Who is Responsible for Corruption in Aid?

World Bank President James Wolfensohn's pronouncement that the 'cancer' of corruption seriously undermines development and will not be tolerated in future Bank funded projects, prompts one to ask: where and when did this corruption originate? How much corruption is acceptable to the World Bank and donor community? For many years the World Bank tended to ignore or discount the significance of corruption in its operations. Donor agencies in general seem to have a very high tolerance for the misuse of their money. Now that the Bank, the UK system, and bilateral agencies are under growing pressure to improve their performance, they are seeking ways to limit the corrupt use of aid money. For the moment, there is little or no evidence that they have any idea of how to go about the task.

One of the main reasons for the disappointing performance of structural adjustment programmes is the misuse of donor money, including systematic corruption. An extreme example is Tanzania's import support programme, which allowed local manufacturers and traders to import raw materials and finished goods. An increasing number of companies, both private and parastatal, began to abuse the system. They stopped paying counterpart funds. Import duty and sales tax were not paid on imports. Neither the Treasury nor the commercial banks had the administrative capacity or the integrity to handle large volumes of free foreign exchange, but the donors ignored the problem. Only when the scandalous behaviour of the banks, the Treasury and the Minister of Finance had reached epic proportions, fuelling inflation and completely derailing the budgetary process, did the World Bank and other donors finally pull the plug on import support.

In December 1996, the IMF started disbursing US$240 million enhanced structural adjustment loan, but to date not one private or parastatal company has been put in receivership for the hundreds of millions of donor dollars which went astray via import support. This casual approach to large-scale corruption has been the norm among donors.

Some bilateral donors have cut the number of countries which they assist, and eradicated funds to those remaining. To increase aid effectiveness some of them have also reduced the number of sectors they support per country. Add to this the tendency for the whole donor community to move into new activities at the same time, and you have a recipe for too much aid chasing too little 'absorptive capacity' in the countries of concentration, which include Tanzania, Uganda and Kenya, Pressure to spend has led to unbelievable over-funding in certain sectors. Well-known examples are NGOs, many of which are created with the sole objective of embezzling donor money.

With the coming of political pluralism, a growing volume of aid money has been channelled into 'governance' activities. The disadvantages of governance from the donor perspective are that donors have little experience in this field, and the amounts of money, which can be disbursed, compared to the amount of administrative work involved, are relatively trivial.

Aid has served to encourage the establishment of a whole range of corrupt activities in 'civil society' to add to those which already existed in the state apparatus. Many of those managing the corruption are recent migrants from the state sector, or straddle both public and private sectors. The politically acceptable employment of more local personnel as desk officers has served to increase the rate of corruption. The chances of being caught or punished are minimal. The few genuine local change-agents are crowded out by the charlatans and opportunists. The imperative to disburse at all costs makes it very difficult for donors to adequately monitor or evaluate the quality of their assistance, since it would put the agencies in a poor light if they were seen to be supporting non-performing and corrupt activities. Thus, as has generally been the case, the donors pretend that their assistance is being well used, and are even prepared to deny well-founded allegations of the misuse of project funds.

The new aid activities discussed above account for a relatively small proportion of total aid flows, however. The basic issue is the amount of uncontrolled corruption which still characterizes the World Bank and other donors' more traditional project, programme, and financial support. Here too one finds projects of ever growing magnitude, as the big spending goes on. The continued availability of donor money is the major determinant of the volume of aid, not performance, structural reform, or impact on 'target groups'. Although further project aid cannot be justified on the basis of past performance, it continues to be a major form of aid delivery by both the World Bank and other donor agencies.

The picture which emerges is that of an oppressed people largely at the mercy of an incompetent and corrupt state apparatus. The role of aid in helping to create and reproduce this lamentable state of affairs is worth exploring. Unfortunately, the report does not mention corruption in aid. If corruption has become one of the major international issues of modern times, it would hardly be surprising to find that the virus has already infected and is spreading within the major agencies.

If countries with as much corruption as Tanzania, Uganda, and Kenya can continue to enjoy billions of dollars of aid every year, it is not because they have demonstrated their ability to use aid wisely. But the donors are not well placed to extol the virtues of transparency and accountability which they do not practice themselves. To address the question of corruption in aid, the World Bank and other agencies will have to take a long look at their own role in creating the problem which they now propose to cure.

9

Challenging Traditional Economic Growth

Today, saving the planet is about redefining our economic development models. Stirving towards the fulfilment of basic human rights is an integral part of environmental protection. Without a people-centred development strategy we will fail. Conflicting interests and lack of vision and courage are among the many reasons why it is so hard to meet needs in a world of plenty. We are faced with three major challenges in the 1990s.

- Top curb population growth and poverty.
- To search for sustainable production and consumption patterns.
- To promote equity.

Population growth is often associated with poverty. But who causes the major strain on the environment? The 1.2 billion poorest people consume small amounts of the world's resources and contribute little to harmful emissions. They do not cause a heavy burden. The day-to-day struggle for survival of the poorest does, however, undermine their resources, and this causes deaths as population grows beyond the carrying capacity of nature. Here two key elements are essential: to turn from non-renewable to renewable resources, and to minize use of resources through resource efficiency. We must single out the products and processes that must be phased out and those which may be allowed to expand. Right prices that include the ecological costs will be explored further, together with administrative measures. We are ready to examine the possibilities of using "green tax" reforms to enhance employment and harness pollution and inefficient resources use. By shifting the burden of taxes from labour to environmentally harmful products and processes we might achieve a double benefit.

Transport, waste management, energy and land use are obvious areas that need to be affected by policy changes. Individuals must use their power as green-conscious citizens and shoppers—but, in the end, producers and service providers hold the main key to practical action.

The market must be harnessed to meet people's needs both for present and future generations—starting by making economic policies play by the rules of nature. The World Trade Organisation (WTO) negotiations have provided us with instruments to regulate world trade.

Getting the Prices Right

Car emissions may be cut drastically, but the rapid increase of new cars nullifies the benefits. Even the most ardent technological optimist must admit that we need new priorities or cuts in some products and services. For example, we must improve public transport and resource-efficient cars—and reduce traffic.

Traditional economic growth models fall short of solving the problem of unemployment. Indeed, 'robots' and wasteful resource use replace people. There are great job-creating possibilities in environment-friendly produces and processes. Striving towards equity within and between nations, and within and between generations, is the major challenge of our time.

The fact that 20 per cent of the world's population consumes 80 per cent of the world's resources has too long been seen as mainly an ethical challenge. Ethics are not easily translated into politics, especially when confronted with economic and market realities. As equity gradually becomes a security issue—as it will, if we do not bridge the gaps within and between nations—it will climb to the top of the political agenda.

Many of the main conflict areas of today are battlefields of resource management. These will expand greatly if we do not turn conference statements of good intention into action. The 30 year old commitment of the rich countries to meet the target of 0.7 per cent of GNP in official Development Assistance remains unmet.

Two hundred years of Western-led development optimism reached its peak in the late 1980s. When the Berlin wall fell, the economic growth models of the rich countries had become the universal recipe. But as more and more people aspire to join the ranks of the middle classes, the resulting environmental stress calls for a halt, or a radical change of course.

The call for new patterns of production and consumption challenges our traditional concepts of economic growth and the focus on materialism in our culture. Neither the industrialised nor the poorer countries are strangers to radical process of change, though the reasons for change are shifting. And we are truly facing challenging and conflict-providing changes.

No nation by itself can solve the problems we face. Pollution knows no frontiers, but comes to us with the winds and waves. We have become more and more interdependent. If we are to attain sustainable development, we must commit ourselves through international agreements, through an international rule of law, through the development of financial mechanisms and through institutional agreements. We must develop means and tools to enhance collective security and mutual interests.

10

Solving the Unemployment Problem by Looking Beyond the Job

If you had a job, you worked; if you didn't, you didn't. Having a job meant being employed by an organisation in a clearly-defined and stable occupational role, with duties, hours, rates of pay and promotion all more or less standardised. But the job-in that meaning of the world—is a social invention, and a fairly recent one.

The job—the kind that you had, or hoped to get-because a central fixture of life. Its importance was great because it served many needs: For managers and efficiency experts, job assignments were the key to assembly-line manufacturing. For union organizers, jobs protected the rights of workers. For political reformers, standardised civil service positions were the essence of good government. Jobs provided an identify the immigrants and recently-urbanised farm workers. They provided a sense of security for individuals and an organising principle for society.

Jobs functioned in so many ways that it is surprising how many organizations are now opting for other ways to define and manage work. The second job shift is underway. Its emergence can be seen in the increasing use of temporary and part-time workers and contracted-out services, the changing relationships between workers and management, the growing popularity of self-employment and small business. Indeed, "de-jobbing" is proceeding at such a pace that many economists, management experts and futurists are now taking freely about the end of the job. Bridges predicts that the job as we now know it will disappear entirely—replaced by new kinds of flexible work assignments in post-job organizations—and be remembered only as a quaint artefact of the industrial age.

One reason for the change in work is the economic rules of the survival game among organizations that employ workers. To stay successful in today's hitech consumer economy, businesses have had to re-model themselves into what some experts call "agile companies"—ones that are able to respond quickly to conditions in ever-changing, fragmenting, competitive markets.

The "knowledge worker", whose work involves not simply doing something, but also applying theoretical or analytical skills. Such workers are replacing the industrial labourer as the dominant part of the workforce—and their productive activities are likely to be organised and structured much differently from those of their assembly-line predecessors.

De-jobbing as a result of new technology or the emergence of a service economy is a phenomenon that gets a lot of attention these days; but it is not the whole story. At all levels of society, people are improvising livelihoods that do not fit the industrial-era model. Immigrants to the developed countries, often unable to find steady jobs, nevertheless find places in the new landscape by being mobile, flexible, resourceful and imaginative: they moonlight, work part-time, share jobs, start small businesses. Their lives are often extremely difficult, but they are also instructive to those of us who believe you either have a job or you're out of luck.

It is too early to evaluate the implications of this multifaceted transformation of work, or to dismiss it as simply good or bad. Nevertheless, one cannot deny that it is taking place, and will bring about dramatic social changes.

On the downside, the job shift is causing great hardships for many workers and their families. It posses serious challenges to policy-makers, political activists and labour leaders. The basic question appears to be whether the key to global employment-development strategy is to play "catch-up"—trying to bring millions of people around the world into jobs in industries and the public sector, or to play "leapfrog"—creating new forms of employment.

The proposal to generate more employment in agriculture, for example, is based on new demand for agricultural exports from developing countries. The policies designed to make the most of this opportunity include measures to upgrade technology, raise productivity, ensure the supply of essential inputs, establish marketing and distribution channels, create links between agriculture and industry, and cater to export markets.

The issue of part-time work, another kind of employment that is seriously undervalued in the traditional industrial era job mind-set. Part time work may not offer much at this point to developing countries, where many people are under employed and wages are low, but it can be of great help in more advanced economies. And it is likely to be a big part of the global work picture in the years ahead.

A certain agility may also be necessary in agriculture, particularly in countries that for many years have depended heavily on producing commodities such as sugar for export as a means of generating income and employment. As Northern laboratories develop non-agricultural substitutes for many of these commodities—and this is already beginning to happen—the bottom may fall out of "monoculture" economies, only economic, but will have long-run political implications as communities attempt to reorganise themselves in response to the changed conditions. It is, therefore, in the interest of raw materials exporters to closely monitor current trends in biotechnology and the use of genetic resources and modify their internal policies in anticipation of potential long-term effects."

This calls for flexibility, and an ability to get information and to act on it. Government officials, development workers, community leaders and individuals will, in some respects, all have to be "knowledge workers" if they are to keep ahead of global changes. Jobs are going to be created not just by putting people to work, but by finding—or creating-new niches where they can be productive.

It is still possible to talk about jobs for all, and to resist the assumption made by many economists that high levels of unemployment are now inevitable. But, as we move ahead into the global information economy, we may be moving back into an older conception of the job, and seeing it again as something you do, rather than as something you have—or that has you.

Crisis Prevention

Can Better Development Planning Lessen the Toll of Civil Emergencies and Natural Disasters?

Even a cursory scan of the world's headlines is depressing: armed conflicts are grinding on in Somalia, Afghanistan and in a growing number of other countries. And the effects of natural disasters are becoming more catastrophic each year. International relief aid, in response to such emergencies, has increased substantially. But how large can these sums of money realistically be expected to grow? With no end in sight to the need for relief, the good will of international donors is quickly giving way to disillusionment.

This leads us to a second question, which is, where does development fit in this grim scenario? For the development community to remain aloof from the issue of disasters and emergencies is not only politically short-sighted, it also ignores totally the causes and the effects of such phenomena.

Natural hazards such as hurricanes and earthquakes may be impossible to prevent. But they only become natural disasters if people are vulnerable. Why is it, for example, that an earthquake in Khilari, Maharashtra that registered 6.9 on the Richter scale killed up to 35,000 people, when an earthquake of almost the exact same magnitude in Los Angeles in 1994 claimed only 57 lives? By reducing poverty we can help increase the coping capacity of vulnerable populations. Therefore helping people lower such vulnerability is as much a development issue as the environment, or women's participation in development. Moreover, the repercussions of natural disasters go far beyond the immediate casualty list that so transfixes the media. Secondary and longer-term effects can be equally if not more devastating. And they must be taken into account by developing practitioners.

It has been estimated, for example, that the damage to Mexico City's infrastructure form a massive 1985 earthquake amounted to US$ 3.6 billion. Yet over the subsequent five years, the negative ripple effect on that country's balance of payments resulted in a loss of $8.6 billion. Furthermore, reconstruction requirements forced Mexican authorities to revise their economic policies to meet an increased demand for public funding, credits and imports. The priorities for public expenditure were redirected to reconstruction projects, leaving many of the pre-disaster problems of the city and its people unattended.

In Bangladesh, floods in the recent past 2,000 people. But on closer examination we find that the toll was much more expensive than that: in each of these years the country's economic growth rate was halved by the delayed planting of rice and the destruction of seedbeds in the floods, further undermining the country's food security. All of these are consideration that go beyond relief, but they must be taken into account by development professionals.

Other emergencies may be more complex, but must be subjected to the same analysis. As the situations in Angola, Burundi, Somalia and the former Yugoslavia demonstrate, we know little about the dynamics of emergencies that arise from civil conflict. We do know, however that their cause usually lies in a lethal mix of poverty, poor governance and ethnic or religious rivalries exacerbated by profound social inequities. We are also learning that their resolution frequently requires the application of peacekeeping and political measures, combined with relief and development.

Among the most virulent effects of such complex emergencies is the massive displacement of people; women and children are the principal victims, constituting 70 per cent of the world's refugees.

These complex emergencies around the world could easily get worse before they get better. This being said, carefully designed development efforts-carried out as building blocks to national reconciliation in the fragile post-conflict stage will need to increase commensurately. The appropriateness and the sustainability of these development efforts will be one of the most important factors in determining whether peace itself becomes sustainable. For example, the absence of carefully tailored reintegration strategies for demobilised soldiers and their host communities would be an almost open invitation to resumed violence.

Yet we must also be conscious of the impact of aid and try harder to prevent the need for relief in the first place. An increasing body of evidence suggests for example that emergency aid can sometimes be counter-productive in the longer term, increasing the vulnerability of populations and impeding recovery. Ironically, we find ourselves in situation today where it is far easier to obtain funds for maintaining refugees in their places of asylum than for helping them reintegrate into their own societies. In such cases, we may very well be helping to perpetuate the problem that we sought to relieve, as the presence of large numbers of refugees is sometimes itself a cause of conflict.

So how are we to proceed? And what exactly is the nature of the relief to development continuum that remains logical in the abstract but elusive in reality? The concept of a continuum does not imply a linear and absolutely progressive set of responses. On the contrary, it means that we are dealing with a set of processes rather than rigidly defined steps. It also means that development must be very much part of the disaster management process, and that the aim of the continuum must be to move from relief to rehabilitation and resumed development at the earliest opportunity. However, this resumed development must include conscious measures to reduce the vulnerability that caused the disaster or the emergency in the first place.

In other words, we must give greater thought to prevention before we reach for the "cure"—for humanitarian, political and financial reasons. (The Japanese insurance industry spends $200 million a year on disaster education alone). And as development practitioners, we must reconcile ourselves to the vastly more complicated environment in which we have to operate.

This means, for example that we will have to begin examining whether the economic policy "medicine" often prescribed will reduce conflict or enhance it. We will have to ask ourselves if the reconstruction period following a civil conflict or natural disaster is the right time to advocate cuts in social spending, as has happened in certain countries in Africa and Latin America. Similarly, is it really in children's best interests to build a school in a seismic zone without first ensuring its structural stability? And does it really make sense to urge drought-prone countries to increase their reliance on cash crops, as has been done in some instances.

A story that never made headlines anywhere involves hundreds of the poorest people in Bangladesh, whose homes remained intact during the floods of 1988, when many others were simply washed away. These people were fortunate enough to have obtained credit through the Grameen Bank for construction materials as well as instruction in the building of flood-resistant homes. The Grameen revolving fund had received start-up capital from International Financial Agencies. Since that time the effort has been expanded, and more than 10,500 flood-resistant homes have been built in the last two years.

This is just one example of the kind of action we need more of—in fairly predictable and recurring circumstances such as the floods in Bangladesh, as well as in the more complex, man-made emergencies to which we must respond.

12

AID Effectiveness as a Multi-Level Process

Parallel to the widespread decrease of aid resources provided by donor countries to developing countries in recent years, debate and research on how to make aid more effective has become a major concern of policy makers and donor aid administrators. Usually, it is suggested that decades of development assistance have at best produced marginal results in terms of improving development levels in the South. Little mention is made of donor's policy shortcomings and the negative impact of these on efforts aimed at reforming and redefining development cooperation in order to enhance aid effectiveness. The policy parameters and operating frameworks of existing and policies continue to inhibit higher degrees of aid effectiveness. In many donor countries, opinion polls indicate waning public support for development aid.

Increasingly, the moral case for aid is called into question and deeper world market integration tends to be seen as the panacea to continue economic decline and social destabilisation in the South. Against this background, cooperation between donor and recipient actors is faced with a duel uphill struggle. First, fewer resources can be mobilised to meet growing developmental needs. On the other hand, to organise and manage development policies and programmes in result oriented manner, grows more difficult. The threat of further aid cuts and of further drops of public support for providing aid become ever more real. A closer look at the organisational complexities and political constraints under which development cooperation is expected to perform effectively may help to improve current aid management approaches.

Towards Conceptual Clarity

At first sight, catchy definitions of what constitutes effective aid might appear attractive to use, in particular with regard to economic indicators, The term "aid effectiveness" is easily used in the same vein as "efficiency", "significance" or "impact" of aid. At times, obsession to measure and demonstrate the results of aid supported development processes can be observed among policy-makers and administrators on the donor side. Still the understanding of aid and its effectiveness as being part and parcel of a cooperation relationship between donor and recipient side parties, is scarcely embedded in practice. To determine how to make aid more effective requires more than a quick impact analysis of an individual and perhaps even isolated development project. Consequently, defining the concept of aid effectiveness needs to take into account at what levels cooperation is focused on. To strive for sustainable and effective modes of development cooperation will entail the need to combine recipient ownership of the development process with donor accountability concerns.

Performance expectations cannot be exclusively placed on the recipient while donor interests, their aid management systems and procedures remain unchanged.

An extended and more analytical, process oriented definition should take into account four main aspects of aid effectiveness:

(a) Effective aid must relate to the building and/or strengthening of in-country aid management capacity:

(b) To maximise the degree of aid effectiveness, local ownership of the aid process is essential: from setting of priorities through policy formulation and implementation on to the evaluation stages of the process;

(c) Increasing recipient side capabilities to take charge of aid relationship, will need to be combined with arrangements to meet legitimate donor accountability concerns;

(d) Aid effectiveness is a two-faceted objective: its realisation is equally dependent on increased transparency of donor motives and on dropping of nondevelopmental, political and economic aid objectiveness of donors.

In addition a broader range of stakeholders in the aid relationship needs to be actively involved: extending beyond accountability government and implementing agencies, to include democratic institutions and organisations of civil society and of the private sector.

Applying any definition of aid effectiveness without disaggregating macro-economic data and taking into account country specificity will only lead to unhelpful generalisations about aid and its effectiveness. It would seen more appropriate to adopt working definitions against which to assess effectiveness of aid resources at a country-specific level. On such a basis one could expect to arrive at more reliable indicators of how well aid resources contribute to improving developmental standards and meeting existing needs.

From Definition to Success—Key Requirements

Having reached agreement between the recipient and donor on what should constitute effectiveness of aid is only a starting point. Embarking on democratic, peaceful and participatory patterns of economic and social development must follow: to arrive at significant and lasting improvements in many of the least developed countries will be a long-term process. This being said, it is crucial to design and implement such forms of development cooperation which involve a wide range of recipient side actors, not only from the government side but also from civil society at large. Seen as a process of increasing inclusion of intended beneficiaries of aid, the commitment to decentralise as well as entrust aid and its management grows in importance.

To fully capture Third World development realities, policy frameworks inspired by neoliberalist-type of development concepts and theories are grossly inadequate. The views and positions on aid articulated in the World Bank and the IMF and others, represent only one side of today's international cooperation, namely the donor side. The major weakness to point out with respect to this locus of debate, is a profound under representation if not even a total absence of recipient experiences and perceptions on aid in general and on its effectiveness in particular. There should be little doubt that ignoring to not actively identifying and involving such perceptions, leads to strongly donor driven aid.

To circumvent recipient side insights and views on strengths and weaknesses of aid strategies and mechanisms, will result in limited local commitment and sense of ownership over the aid process. Mutual decision-making between donors and recipients remains a rare policy approach. Aid procedures that are based on local management and less control-oriented donor roles in the aid process are still exceptions in development cooperation.

Structurally, in terms of the policy environment within which development aid is expected to function, the overriding policy framework is general based on structural adjustment policies (SAP). But the underlying conclusion made by proponents of SAPs that these policies induce aid effectiveness, has yet to be proven valid. It must suffice at this point to emphasize that there is not a priori relationship between world market integration under structural adjustment and sustainable development in poor countries. Aid to these countries which is solely intended to reinforce fundamentally uneven and unequal patterns of world market integration should at be scrutinised critically.

Some central issues need to be addressed in the course of improving aid and its effectiveness:

- institutional dimensions of aid relationships require strong policy-attention, both on the donor and the recipient side;
- capacities to effectively identify and formulate aid priorities need to be strengthened in recipient countries;
- local capacities to sustain reform efforts must be reinforced.

Levels of Intervention

If the design of aid and the terms upon which it is provided to a developing country are largely determined by the donor, the aid relationship can be characterised as essentially hierarchical. Recipient side views will rarely surface, as they are either not identified, or not well formulated. Possibilities of a recipient-led development strategies can be limited. Unless scope is provided to the recipient side actors to assume responsibilities, aid effectiveness is likely to remain low or fluctuating, and the sustainability of donor aid efforts will remain doubtful.

National planning processes and courses of national development in recipient countries should be seen as most effective where they are led under local responsibility and control. To arrive at this ideal situation, gaps need to be reduced and closed at the various intervention levels.

Donor aid resources provide valuable support for this process. Their effectiveness in meeting long-term objective of aid will need to be assessed on the basis of how well they perform at the different levels. Individual donors will expectedly perform differently at the various levels. What will prove to be the ultimate test for effectiveness is how well the donor aid performance accomplishes the broader objectives of development cooperation and how well it includes sustainable results.

In the analytical frameworks outlined here, development cooperation would seem to be confronted with the effectiveness gaps at the:

- structural level: International trade and investment patterns, debt problems and world market integration process appear as long-term constraining factors upon aid and its effectiveness;
- at the policy level, dialogue and partnership in development cooperation are instrumental factors in recluding planning and co-ordination gaps with regard to policy analysis and formulation;
- The institutional level is where pertinent capacity gaps exist: capacity development efforts of donors and technical assistance measures play an important role in addressing weaknesses in aid effectiveness within a country's institutional setting;
- finally, at the level of aid projects (programmes), it is generally the lack of sustainability of aid interventions which causes development activities to falter once donor support decreases or stops. In addition to technical cooperation, financial and material inputs serve to maintain project momentum and goal realisation: the issue of how to develop local capacity sufficiently in order for indigenous organisations to continue project activities initially supported by donor aid, remains the most important issue to address at this level.

Fostering aid Effectiveness

In recent years donor aid budgets have been reshuffled while having decreased in real terms. Geographical redistributions of reduced aid budgets have been accompanied by the need to accommodate rising emergency needs.

Additional resources to meet these needs have not been forthcoming: in general, aid budgets destined for development purposes have been under severe pressures while urgent humanitarian needs have added to the drain on resources.

Donor and recipient development efforts are too often isolated from one another, or poorly coordiantted. They fail to address managerial and implementation bottlenecks. Cross-sectorial linkages, as well as interdisciplinary approaches to aid problems are only slowly gaining ground. It is increasingly obvious, that decisions on aid issues are subjected to concerns outside of the responsible ministry: finance ministers, economics ministers and unfortunately even defence ministers have a strong say in how much aid is to be provided, where it is to be concentrated and under what terms to be utilised. Inside of recipient countries, large portions of national budgets are allocated to non-development priorities with little or no impact on alleviating urgent poverty problems.

Development cooperation may make the biggest impact and be executed most effectively where donors and recipients agree upon multi-level aid strategies. To give an example: building a road to a remote rural area may well be done in an effective project manner: it is equally important to have a functioning transport authority in place to ensure maintenance of the roads. If this authority operates within a nationally defined infrastructure policy, best in accord with national trade and investment priorities, then the effectiveness of the project-level road building programme has a good chance of being high.

Institutional changes to set the stage for a profound reform process in development cooperation are needed. Reprioritising national budgets to reflect identified in country development needs may be one step. Setting up policy evaluation and formulation units can be complimentary measures. Deregulating markets and investment rules may serve to please donors, but dumping of cheap products which strangle local production efforts may easily result. Regional cooperation, including intensified South-South cooperation can provide some counterbalance. There are only a few areas where changes in the current system of development cooperation can occur, with a view to better manage the complexities of aid and the social,

What future food security will look like depends not on exogenous factors over which we have no control but on the decisions and actions taken by the major players: households, private and public sector agencies, governments, and the international community. If we continue to act as we have in the 1980s and early 1990s, more people will suffer from food insecurity it will be because some or all of these players failed to act in an appropriate and timely manner.

Feeding the World: Availability and Access to Food

There is enough food in the world today to feed everyone, if it were evenly distributed. Availability of daily food energy per capita in the developing countries as a whole increased by 0.7 per cent per year during the 1980s.

Twenty-five developing countries, including about half of the African countries, were unable to assure sufficient food energy (2,200 calories per person per day) for their populations at the end of the 1980s even if available food energy were evenly distributed within each country. This is down from 45 countries at the end of the 1970s.

However, available food is neither evenly distributed nor fully consumed. Availability of enough food at global, regional, or national levels does not necessarily mean that everyone is well fed. For people to be food secure—that is, to have access at all times to the food required for a healthy and productive life—there must be both availability of food and access to food. Access to food by households (and individuals) is conditioned by poverty: the poor usually lack adequate means to secure access to food.

Over 1.1 billion people in developing countries were living in poverty in 1993, more than 500 million in conditions of extreme poverty. South Asia is the home of about 50 per cent of the developing world's poor—more than 500 million people. Another 15 per cent are found in East Asia, 19 per cent in sub-Saharan Africa, and 10 per cent in Latin America and the Caribbean. The prevalence of poverty (the proportion of each region's population that is poor) is very high—about 50 per cent—in South Asia as well as in sub-Saharan Africa.

Today, there are more than 700 million people who do not have access to sufficient food to meet their needs for a healthy and productive life; they often go hungry, adults and children also suffer from diseases associated with hunger and poverty. For almost one fifth of the total population of developing countries to be chronically hungry tarnishes the images of a world that is now considered food-secure because it produces enough food.

Great progress has been made in meeting food needs during the last 30 years. For instance, the number of underfed people declined from an estimated 976 million in 1974-76 to 786 million in late 1980s. But the problem is far from solved. Keeping up with increasing needs and demands due to population growth, income increases, and dietary changes is itself a formidable challenge.

Hunger and food insecurity have a significant effect on health and nutrition of both adults and children. They can lead to growth failure in children. About 184 million pre-school children in developing countries were underweight in 1994. About 55 per cent of these underweight children were found in South Asia and another 16 per cent in sub-Saharan Africa. The proportion of children that are underweight is higher in South Asia (almost 60 per cent), but it is also significant in Sub-Saharan Africa (30 per cent) and Southeast Asia (31 per cent). It is worrisome that the number of underweight children in Sub-Saharan Africa during the 1980s from 20 million to 28 million is particularly striking.

In addition to energy deficiencies, micro nutrient deficiencies are also widespread in the developing world. About 14 million pre-school children (under the age of five years) have eye damage as a result of Vitamin-A deficiency. Ten million of these children are found in Southeast Asia. Between 250,000 and 500,000 pre-school children go blind each year due to Vitamin-A deficiency, two-thirds of these children die within months of going blind. Many more children are mildly affected. Recently research has shown that even mild deficiencies can increase mortality significantly. Vitamin-A deficiencies are closely linked to diet, which can be influenced by agricultural research and policy.

Iron deficiency affects about 1 billion people in the world. particularly children and women of reproductive age. Iron deficiency leads to anaemia, which if not checked can diminish learning capacity and increase morbidity and morality. In the developing countries, about 370 million women between 15 and 49 years of age—42 per cent of this population group—were anaemic in the 1980s. Almost one-half were in South Asia. And there are tentative indications from South Asia and sub-Saharan Africa that the prevalence of anaemia is rising in non pregnant adult women of reproductive ages.

In Sub-Saharan Africa, this trend is undoubtedly associated with deterioration in general standards of living, including increased poverty and food insecurity. Anaemia partly arises from diets insufficient in iron, which again could be addressed through agricultural research and policy. For example, a possible reason why iron deficiency and anaemia are going up in South Asia may lie in the decrease in production of iron rich pulses during that same period, which in part reflects the larger research input into competing crops such as wheat in South Asia. This emphasizes the importance of considering the effects on diet and thus on health and nutrition in setting research priorities for yield-increasing research.

South Asia is the home of about half of the developing world's hungry and food-insecure people, but this population group is growing rapidly in Sub-Saharan Africa. Much of the poverty and food insecurity is in rural areas, mainly in low-potential areas such as arid zones, but urban poverty is also growing rapidly.

Four Key Factors will Influence Future Food Production and Consumption

Global and regional food production and consumption during the next 10-20 years will be influenced by a large number of factors. Changes in the following four sets of factors are likely to particularly important:

1. Economic growth and economic policies;
2. Population growth and urbanisation;
3. Rural infrastructure, agricultural production technology, and access to modern inputs; and
4. Natural resource management and environmental consideration.

The expected impact of each of these factors on future food production and consumption is considerable.

Economic Growth and Economic Policies

Economic growth must resume in the developing world, especially in Sub-Saharan Africa. To support such growth, it is critical to:

- complete structural adjustment and economic reforms;
- remove external barriers to growth such as trade distortions and subsidies in developed countries;
- liberalize trade and remove market distortions;
- enhance access by the poor to land, capital, and technology;
- expand investment in rural infrastructure, health, education, and agricultural research and technology;
- facilitate sustain ability in agricultural production; and
- reverse the decline in international assistance to agriculture.

Growth in real per capita income during the 1980s was disappointing for developing countries as a whole. However, the low average rate of growth covers large variations among regions. The high rates of economic growth in Asia are expected to continue through the 1990s, while incomes in Sub-Saharan Africa are expected to keep pace with population growth.

Future economic growth depends on internal policies as well as on the international policies as well as on the international environment. The extent to which current structural adjustment and economic reforms in Latin America, Sub-Saharan Africa, the Commonwealth of Independent States (CIS), Eastern Europe, and selected countries in Asia and the Middle East are carried to successful completion at an appropriate speed and sequence is of paramount importance for future economic growth in those countries.

Closely related to this issue is the question of the most appropriate role of the stable in a market-oriented economy with inappropriate institutions, poor infrastructure, and insufficient experience by the private sector in dealing effectively in a competitive market environment. Overreaction to past failures such as excessive and inappropriate state intervention may cause governments to take on a passive role where intervention is needed to assure that the markets function effectively and to deal with outside influences on the economy.

Future economic growth will also depend on the international trade environment, including trade distortions by developed countries, and access to external aid. Import restrictions for agricultural and non-agricultural products in Japan, the European Union, and the United States, along with domestic agricultural subsidies and implicit and explicit export subsidies for agricultural products, are of particular concern.

Population Growth and Urbanisation

If progress in economic growth is not to be undermined by rapid population growth and excessive urbanisation, effective population and migration policies are necessary to complement growth-oriented policies. Such policies must focus on:

- universal access to family planning information and technology; and
- incentives to reduce rural-urban migration, such as provision of employment in rural areas and stimulation of agricultural and non-agricultural growth in rural areas.

Although the annual growth rate is falling for the world as a whole, the population increase during the next 20-30 years, of slightly less than 100 million people a year, will be the largest ever. Approximately 97 per cent of this increase is projected to occur in the Third World, with Africa alone accounting for 34 per cent of the growth. Thus although reductions in annual population growth rates have begun to occur in Asia and Latin America, they are insufficient to counter the absolute increases. Population growth rates of these magnitudes will greatly increase the need for food and other basic necessities.

Rural Infrastructure, Agricultural Production Technology, and Access to Modern Inputs

Continued progress in all three of these areas is critical to future food security.

- Resources must be committed to infrastructure construction and maintenance. Labour-intensive public works programmes are a viable mechanisms for building roads, reforesting areas, and engaging in soil conservation projects, while creating employment and income in rural areas.
- International and national agricultural research must continue to develop yield-enhancing production technology, especially in maize, millet, and other crops, as well as build tolerance or resistance in crops to pests and adverse climatic conditions.

- Farmer access to modern inputs must be facilitated through provision of credit and technical assistance. Inputs must be made available to all farmers on time and in required amounts.

The importance of investments in rural infrastructure within the context of rapid urbanisation has already been established. Even without rapid urban growth, however, such investments are needed in many developing countries, particularly the poorest ones, to facilitate agricultural and rural development. Improved rural infrastructure enhances access to export markets, modern production inputs, and consumer goods. It reduces marketing costs, promotes exchange between intracountry markets, reduces spatial and temporal price distortions, and, in general, increases efficiency in production and marketing.

However, while essential, effective rural infrastructure alone is not enough to assure agricultural and rural development and rapid increases in food production in developing countries. Yield enhancing production technology is of critical importance. Although opportunities for expansion of agricultural production into lands not currently under cultivation still exist in some countries, such opportunities are so limited that they would probably not be able to counter losses of current agricultural lands to alternative uses on a global level. Furthermore, attempts to expand agricultural production into new lands would, in most cases, require large investments in technology, tools and materials and would increase the risk of land degradation and deforestation. Thus, future increases in food production must come primarily from higher yields per unit of land rather than from land expansion.

Agricultural research has successfully developed yield-enhancing technology for the majority of crops grown in temperate zones and for several crops grown in tropical zones. The dramatic impact of agricultural research and modern technology on wheat and rice yields in Asia and Latin America since the mid-1980s is well known. Less dramatic but significant yield gains have been obtained from research and technological change in other crops, particularly maize.

Natural Resource Management and Environmental Considerations

Research, technology development, incentives, and regulations are needed to prevent environmental degradation. These measures include appropriate water management policies, reduction of subsidies that encourage wasteful use of inputs better definition of ownership and user rights to resources including land, education of farmers to encourage appropriate use of technology and resource conservation, and the provision of alternatives to resource-degrading inputs and techniques. Since poverty is a major source of degradation, poverty eradication is justified also on environmental grounds.

The recent surge in public and private concerns about negative environmental effects of economic growth and development may, if sustained, have important implications for agricultural development and future food production and consumption. Of particular concern of the need to avoid degradation of natural resources such as land and water, as well as deforestation, water contamination, and health risks associated with the use of chemicals. Since most of the current and potential resource degradation and environmental contamination result from situations in which those who cause and possibly benefit from degradation do not pay the costs, neither the market nor the individual producers and consumers are likely to incorporate preventive measures into their behaviour. Only when sufficient damage has been done to influence significantly current or future production costs will market and producer behaviour change. The state is more likely to undertake preventive measures either through publicly funded research and technology development or through incentive policies and regulations. Extensive water logging, salination, and associated land degradation and productivity losses resulting from inappropriate water management are of particular concern in large parts of Asia.

No Time for Complacency

Population growth will outstrip growth in food production in Sub-Saharan Africa for a long time to come unless more is done to accelerate agricultural growth. Between now and 2000, the population will grow at more than 3 per cent a year, while food production is likely to grow at 2 per cent or less a year. By the year 2000, the production shortfall is estimated to increase to about 50 million tons of grain equivalent, up from the current level of about 14 million tons. The region will not have the necessary foreign exchange to import such large amounts of food. And Africa governments will not be able to count on enough food aid to make up the difference. If current trends continue, by the year 2020, Africa will have a food shortage of 250 million tons, which is more than 20 times the current food gap.

Poverty is expected to increase rapidly in the coming years. Sub-Saharan Africa's share of the world's poor is expected to increase from the current 19 per cent to about 28 per cent in 2000. Furthermore, the number of underweight children in expected to increase in the 1990's in Sub-Saharan Africa.

Asian demand for cereals is estimated to grow at an annual rate of 2.1 per cent between now and the year 2000, where as food production is expected to grow at 1.9 per cent per year. Much of the production shortfall is likely to be dealt with through expanded imports and perhaps through expanded regional production in response to price increases.

In Latin America, by contrast, growth in food production is anticipated to exceed food demand growth: food production is estimated to grow by 3 per cent annually between 1990 and 2000, while food demand is estimated to grow by 2.5 per cent per year.

Large areas of land are rapidly being degraded and deforested. And the principal reasons for environmental degradation—poverty, high population growth, and limited access to appropriate agricultural technology—are not being dealt with effectively.

About 700 million people are food insecure for them the food crisis has arrived. For the 10-12 million preschool children who died in 1994 from hunger and diseases related to malnutrition, the food crisis came and went. One-third of the preschool children of the Third World are unable to grow to their full potential and face increased risk of death and disease.

Complacency is not in order. Clearly, Malthus underestimated the power of science to expand food production. The mass starvation that was predicted for Asia in the 1970s and 1980s did not occur because science was effectively put to work to expand crop yields. However, past yield increases came about people with foresight made appropriate decisions. The failure to expand investments in agricultural research and technology development during the 1980s and 1990s indicates that such foresight no longer prevails. Given the long lag time between investment in agricultural research and the resulting production increases, failure to invest today will show up in production shortfalls 10 to 20 years from now. The problems associated with environmental degradation will present themselves sooner. We must not wait until a global food crisis is upon us or until the last tree has fallen to make these investments.

REFERENCES

1. FAO, FAO Production Yearbook.
2. FAO, "The State of Food and Agriculture 1992".
3. FAO, "Agriculture Towards 2010".
4. FAO, "The State of Food and Agriculture 1994".
5. FAO, Food Outlook (December 1994).
6. World Bank, World Development Report 1995.

7. World Bank, Global Economic Prospects and the Developing Countries.

8. World Food Programme, Food Aid in Review (Rome WFP 1992).

9. World Bank, Global Economic Prospects and the Development Countries 1992. (Washington, D.C.: World Bank).

14

What's Driving Migration

The scale and diversity of today's migrations are beyond any previous experience. Rapid urban growth and environmental degradation in rural areas have led to internal migration affecting hundreds of millions of people. Migration is now seen as a priority issue equal in political weight to other major global challenges such as the environment, population growth and economic imbalances between regions.

Families and households form the basis for economic growth, social development and personal fulfilment. Decisions, by individual women and men on marriage, family, a place to live, shape the destinies of communities and nations. National policies and international conditions provide the context for individual decision-making. Effective development policies, including population, reproductive health and family planning policies, address this reality.

Data on national and global population trends set the agenda for national policy. An important element of population programmes is gathering data that will allow policy-making responsive to the realities of daily life, and to the needs and aspirations of individuals.

The dominant feature of global demographics is still growth. Age distribution is a growing concern, as the numbers of young and elderly people, grow, relative to the working-age population. The world is growing steadily more urban. From being a sign of strength and dynamism in the national economy, the rate and scale of urban growth has become increasingly a cause for concern. The influx of migrants to the biggest cities may be weakening both urban and rural sectors.

International migration is small in extent compared with internal movements, but has a disproportionate impact. Both internal and international migration are driven by population growth, and by inequities between countries. Migration is one of the choices which shape people's lives and the destiny of nations. But it can also be a symptom of inequity and underdevelopment. Migrants are by definition the most vulnerable members of the host community. Their living and working conditions should be protected.

Open and frank exchange of information and views between host and sending countries is needed more than ever. The aim of the international community should be to protect the right to move, but to ensure that movement is voluntary and that it stimulates rather than holds back personal and national development. "The point of departure should be the human right to live and work where one pleases, so long as it does not infringe on other people's rights to do the same."

The Urban Transformation

The rural sector is declining in importance and its contribution to national economies. It is increasingly part of a unified economy based on the city. Contact with the urban areas is easier than ever and is encouraged by rural development.

Temporary and circular migration is giving way to more permanent settlement. The largest cities are under increasing strain, and residents are encountering increasing difficulties in improving or even maintaining living conditions. Nevertheless, migration continues, driven by a variety of forces both positive and negative. The choice to move can be part of a strategy for survival or personal development; but it is often enforced by external conditions.

The urban transformation is irreversible, but the rural sectors must also be strengthened to balance the developing economy. Attention to gender issues will be crucial in ensuring a successful transition. The forces driving internal and international migration have much in common. Demographic pressures are contributing to both. As the pressures encouraging migration increase, the options for migrants become more limited. This collision is contributing to the atmosphere of crisis surrounding both urban and international migration.

Costs and Benefits

Migration is the result of individual or family decisions. But it is also part of social process. In economic terms, migration is as much a global phenomenon as trade in commodities or manufactured goods. It is part of a broader pattern, and evidence of changing economic, social and cultural relationships.

But migration may be evidence of a different kind of relationship; the combination of poverty, rapid population growth and environmental damage is a powerful destabilizing factor driving urban growth and eventually international migration. On the recipient side, migration has usually been seen as evidence of a thriving economy; today's industrial states were built in part by migrant labour, skills and investment. In today's increasingly uncertain conditions, migration may be seen as a threat to the security and well-being of the local workforce and society at large.

The only effective means to reduce migration pressures over the long term are to slow population growth; to stimulate economic growth and job creation at home, and promote the development of the individual and the family as the basic economic and social unit.

A Question of Gender

It is often assumed that most migrants are men, in reality, women make up nearly half of the international migrant population. Gender differences in social and economic roles affect migration decision making, household strategy, and the sex composition of labour migration. Attention to the gender dimension of migratory movements ought to be an important component in population and development planning.

Women frequently take the initiative in migration decisions, which may reflect limited opportunities in rural areas. Low status limits women's choices at home and may increase pressure to migrate, but it may also affect life in the host community. Opportunities may be limited by lack of education or skills, or by customer limitation on women's freedom of action outside the family or ethnic group. Paid employment for migrant women is usually in the lowest wage, least secure, and lowest status jobs, mostly in housework, child care and trade.

Most educated women end up in the same low-status, low-wage production and servicejobs as unskilled female migrants. Men too, experience downward mobility, but the contrast in the decline in women's employment status is far greater. Despite these disadvantages women migrants have become significant economic actors. Their status may be improved by migration, but the advantages are not clear-cut. Women's status as migrants is affected by their vulnerability, and by their lack of reproductive freedom. To ensure improved status they will need both legal protection and essential services, including reproductive health services.

Refugees

Refugees in the 1990s are overwhelmingly in Asia, Africa and Latin America. Their numbers are large, about 17 million, and growing rapidly. A further 3.5 to 4 million were thought to be in "refugee-like situations", though estimates are probably extremely conservative, and an estimated 23 million people internally displaced.

It is important to recognize the common roots of refugees and other forms of mass movement of populations.

At the same time, despite the difficulty of distinguishing between political and socio-economic causes of migration, there is a clear need to distinguish between refugees and other groups of migrants. Participation in international efforts of burden-sharing would ensure that most refugee problems would be dealt with in their regions of origin.

Conclusions and Policies

Migration highlights linkages and interdependencies within countries, with many implications for development agendas, including population programmes and development assistance.

Policies to regulate or moderate international migration have concentrated largely on urban growth. They have been only intermittently effective. The most successful have concentrated on stimulating rural development and the growth of alternative urban centres

Migration is also a personal or family decision, which is affected by external conditions such as poverty or environmental degradation, improving conditions of personal and family life can make a crucial difference in the decision to migrate, reducing dependence on migration as a strategy. Because migration is the result of personal and family decisions, it can be influenced by policies that improve the quality of life.

This offers the opportunity for policies emphasizing individual development, among them education, health (including reproductive health) and family planning. Such policies are particularly relevant to the strategies must take into account gender differences in social and economic life and the differential effects of policies.

Migration decisions are about family security and long-term-life-chances, rather than simply the maximisation of income. They are ultimately strategies designed to look after the individual's and the household's needs, safeguard their security, and respond to their aspirations. If the goal is to reduce migration pressures through development it will be essential to increase the capacity but reduce the need to migrate. Long-term external support will be required to make such policies a reality, particularly in areas of rapid population growth and potential mass outward flows. Highly co-ordinated allocation of development assistance can help establish priorities and focus attention on basic needs. The challenge to both international donors and co-operating governments is to direct programme spending to the areas where it can be most effective.

15

Equal Opportunities for Women in the Community

Over half the people in the Indian community are women. The change in women's contribution to society is one of the most striking phenomena of the late twentieth century. But although they have had the law behind them, women have yet to enjoy the equality they are entitled to in theory. Men need to contribute more to family life, while women have yet to make a real impact on decisions affecting the lives of everybody.

Technological advances have meant the decline of employment in manufacturing, and the growing dominance of service industries. This has meant more jobs for women, but not necessarily better working conditions. Most women are still in lower-paid jobs, and most still work mainly with other women in similar jobs and fields. Women are still under-represented in many sectors of industry, the professions and public service.

More and more women are involved in paid work. There is no job they cannot do, and they are entitled to equal pay for equal work, as well as the same terms and conditions at work, and the same opportunities for promotion. Giving women the opportunity to realise their potential in all spheres of society is increasingly important, for only by involving both sexes to the full can we develop human resources on really democratic lines.

Equal Pay, Equal Opportunities

The right to equal pay for equal work without discrimination based on sex has to be set out. Equal treatment in access to employment, training, promotion and working conditions has to be encouraged. Equal treatment in social security, as well as for the self-employed are very much needed. Rights to maternity leave and pay and a guarantee of adequate health and safety at work for pregnant women and nursing mothers are urgent. The government has to encourage good practice on: Positive action, vocational training, childcare, combating unemployment, equal opportunities in schools, integrating women into working life, combating unwanted sexual behaviour at work, education, and updating protective legislation affecting women.There is still a great deal to be done before we can claim women in the community really get a fair deal and a chance to show what they can do.

Women are still often segregated into jobs that are less well-paid than those typically taken by men. They are often well qualified than men, and the jobs they do are often less secure. These are the kinds of inequalities the society must continue to combat and it will do so, as one of the ways of making sure women do not bear the brunt. Quality and quantity in women's employment is very important.

Better Opportunities to Earn a Living

Getting more women into paid work by promoting job opportunities, entrepreneurship and local employment should be the aim. The aim should be to help them fulfil their potential through better education, training and positive action. Upgrading their skills and equipping them with hi-tech know-how is a priority. Another major concern is helping parents juggle work and caring responsibilities via better services and terms of employment.

Getting Women in Positions of Power

It is hard to believe over half the community's population is female, given how little direct influence women have over what happens in our society. In an electoral constituency where half the voters are women, and where concerns for education, family health and food are paramount, both contestants up for election are male, and they speak to a largely male audience. The women, who work long hours and worry and sacrifice for their families and homes, fuss with the tea, hush the children up are on the periphery. If they are there at all. Polictics is 'men's business'.

Training to Keep up with the Times

Women need training if they are to benefit from growth and technological development. A network of training schemes have to be set up to develop training for women, to publicise their needs, promote information exchanges and encourage the involvement of employers and trade unions.

Changing Minds in School

There is no job women cannot do. A working party is looking at ways of encouraging boys and girls to range more widely in the subjects they take in school. It should aim to support teachers trying to avoid reproducing anachronistic stereotypes.

Pregnant women, mothers of new-born babies and nursing mothers should have the peace of mind of knowing they have secure health and social rights. For women who already have to combine their professional life with running a home and looking after children, political activity requires considerable sacrifice. Woman would be more ready to take them on if they thought they stood a chance of recognition on a par with men. That is far from being the case. If equal opportunities for women are provided definitely the country will develop at faster rate.

16

Trade and Labour Standards

Using the Wrong Instruments for the Right Cause

A moral value is a shared concern of humanity; hence its enforcement should be a cooperative task implemented for the benefit of humankind. Would we qualify recent approaches to the issue of trade and labour standards as non-inquisitory but shared and cooperatives ones? The purpose of this brief is to shed some light on this question.

In fact, nobody, will deny any country the right to raise and fight for issues which are of moral concern for humanity, as they are supposed to benefit humankind. The issue of implementing and enforcing a core of labour standards one of these.

However, a problem remains: who has the negotiating power to raise and impose them? The key issue is that trade coercive attempts by some become inquisitorial as soon as they are backed by moral concerns which are supposed to be shared by all while the same "all" lack the negotiating power to be, in turn, coercive if they so wish. In other words, trade related coercion forcedly becomes "inquisition" when moral concerns are introduced into the functioning of an international trading system characterized by large imbalances in the negotiating power of the participating countries. Only a few Governments have the negotiating leverage and strength to develop what we may qualify as "trade-related inquisitory practices".

The issue of trade and labour standards seems to have arisen when "uniform competition" has been regarded as a

threat to employment and economic growth in some industrial countries.

However, without attaining a certain degree of international agreement and coherence as to whether and under what conditions—a given competitive advantage is, or is not, related to social or other conditions, and whether or not it may be considered as "unfair". With protectionist view in mind, such an approach may only be interpreted as "unbending thinking" coming from "unfair competitiveness seekers".

If the motivation behind the introduction and further use of moral argumentation is to seek a justification for the possible use of trade measures as enforcement mechanisms to achieve certain goals. Particularly for harmonisation of labour standards, one may wonder why the labour standards issue has not been linked to North-North trade in the current debate on the considerable variation in labour standards among developed countries. The motivation may well be that in the post-Uruguay Round era, when tariffs have been reduced substantially and "grey area measures" put under stricter control or even banned, We may be facing the possible revival of new forms of protectionism wearing "blue", "green" or "multicolour" masks. On the contrary, if the motivation behind the introduction of such moral labour rights argumentation reflects a real commitment by the international community to enforce labour standards, a door may be open for embarking, in the future, on a series on international initiatives, not necessarily under the trade umbrella.

It should also be stressed that the linkage between trade and labour standards has been seriously misinterpreted. Most analysts remain blind to the two-way character of the link between trade and labour standards. On the one hand, trade liberalisation is to promote growth and development by promoting a more efficient allocation of resources and to ease the adoption and implementation of labour standards, as well as to promote job creation. On the other hand—and this is extremely important—raising labour standards—not keeping them low-should increasingly be seen as the real source of competitiveness and economic growth through, among others, increase in the quality of labour. There is a case for considering economic progress and the rise in labour standards as mutually reinforcing.

Turning to the low labour standard debate, much more empirical and analytical evidence is needed to asses the extent to which low labour standard are correlated to lower wages and labour costs. Although raising labour standards may not primarily be intended to maximize efficiency, it is becoming increasingly evident that efficiency and the future potential of the firm may not necessarily be maximized by keeping labour standards low. In this context, it is the development to human capital in LDCs which is a top priority, not because failing to respect labour standards in these economies threatens the welfare of the workers in the industrialized countries but, more simply, because it is the only strategy for enhancing the productivity of labour and ultimately increasing the people's standard of living. Thus, if raising labour standards and ensuring their effective implementation is important for economic progress, developed and developing countries, as well as wokers and employers in each region, should adopt a cooperative, not cofrontational, approach in order to deal with this urgent and pressing problem. For this very reason, adherence to trade sanctions would be a wrong approach. Trade is essential for enhancing woker's productivity because it ensures that a country's resources will be employed in the activities that it is best at, In turn, increased productivity is the key to development, higher labour standards and higher wages. Moreover, the issue of labour standards is of a moral nature: it has an undeniable development dimension which needs to be more clearly perceived but, as discussed, it is certainly not an issue to be dealt with through trade measures.

Labour standards should be dealt with in the WTO. The Capacities of the ILO will prove invaluable for renewed multilateral effort to improve working conditions in developing countries. Its tripartite structure has proved to be the best suited to the tasks of conciliation and dialogue.

Improving the standards of living and labour standards for workers or eradicating child labour is what matters it is the right cause for humankind, a cause to fight for, through various approaches and by using all the mechanisms at our disposal in order to ensure its success. Thus, the issue is not one of trade and labour standards, but of labour standards and economic development, an issue of a human dignity and human rights nature. It is a universal issue, the solutions to which should be found by all nations, taking into account equity considerations. Each country should participate in the process, depending on its level of economic development. It is precisely because economic development, including trade, is positively correlated with the adoption and effective implementation of labour standards that solutions to low labour standards should not necessarily come from negative and coercive approaches. Solutions for universal problems must not only be efficiency-based but also equity-based. Therefore, the case is for cooperation rather than coercion and for applying positive instruments. As in the case of environmental issues, developing countries should be recipients of funds, technical cooperation and other similar forms of support when the implementation of labour standards involves an inequitable cost burden.

The initiative of "grouping" a core of existing conventions into a new global convention on core labour standards of universal value may, in view of its new and distant qualitative nature, generate strong support from the international community for its implementation. The ILO was created to promote workers' right, so the initiative could be launched under its aegis, in direct collaboration with other intergovernmental organisations dealing with social, trade and development issues in an interrelated manner. The support to this or other similar approaches by the international community, and in particular by those developed countries that have recently shown a special and strong interest in the reinforcement and implementation of labour rights in developing countries, will be a clear sign of their dergree of sincerity and their willingness to share the social concerns of universal value which seem to be of paramount interest to most of their citizens.

17

The Dematerialisation of the World Economy

The first Industrial Revolution marked the transition from robber-and-plunder colonialism to the systematic development of the "overseas" territories in the framework of the international division of labour between raw materials suppliers and manufacturers of finished goods. There was an "historic integration" of the colonised areas in the development of their parent-states. What will the third Industrial Revolution do for the Third World ? Will it now come to an "historic separation" ?

The end of the East-West conflict was reason enough to talk about a radical change in world politics. But at the same time an upheaval in the world economy is taking place that possibly will have even wider impacts. As a reference point for the following thoughts, three dimensions of this change are pointed out:

1 The upgrading of processing information rather than materials as object of economic activity (technological dimension) ;

2 the evolvement of global communications networks (sociocultural dimension) ;

3 the change of the nature of work (socio-economic dimension).

All three dimensions can be summarised under the buzzphrase "tertialisation of the world economy."

In that respect, talk of the "Third Industrial Revolution" is misleading. It is not about a third epoch of industrialisation, but about the beginning of a de-industrialisation, the transition from the industrial to the information society.

Historic Separation?

In the 1960s and early 1970s, there was often talk of the Third World as the Third Sector of the world economy. Also then the Third World was not much more than an "imaginary community". But as such it had a certain significance in world politics. This implied not only its strategic role in the East-West conflict and its ideological function as the supporter of different "third paths" between capitalism and socialism. It was also about the Third World's attested "chaos power". That linked the fear (in the North) and the hope (in the South) that the developing countries would be in a position to cut off the industrial nations from supplies of important raw materials, thus putting them under pressure. But it was soon seen that both sides had over estimated this possibility, even with regard to oil. Instead of supply bottlenecks arising, raw materials prices plummeted. For some commodities, the fall in prices exceeded those of the Great Depression of 1929/30.

This was due, inter alia, to the conjunction of lower demand from the industrial nations and expansion of production by the raw materials suppliers. Business activities dependent upon the supply of raw materials are tending to lose importance compared with the overall development of the global economy. The reason for this is to be seen in the transition from a material to an information economy.

This transition is taking place in line with the revolutionizing of data transmission and the expansion of financial transactions which are not directly related to changes in the production of materials. The speed of the changes is remarkable.

However, the dematerialisation of business activities does not lead to decoupling of the Third World from the world economy. Declining market shares in world trade are not the expression of separation, but a loss of the affected countries positions in the world economy. Thus, the impact of dematerialisation is "only" that the negotiating positions of raw materials suppliers vis–a–vis the industrial nations will deteriorate further.

Differentiation of the Third World

But the radical change in the global economy is affecting some developing countries worse than others. Sub–Saharan Africa, and some countries in West and South Asia and Latin America are being pushed back further. The oil–producing countries with their high per capita export earnings will be able to hold their positions in the world economy for some time to come. The threshold countries of East and South-East Asia can expand theirs so long as they can continue to attract a growing share of global industrial production, and at the same time participate in the tertialisation of the world economy in the shape of rapidly-growing financial transactions. Thereby it should be noted that the degree of tertialisation in itself is not an adequate indicator for economic avant-gardism. Brazil exhibits a high degree of tertialisation in combination with a low macroeconomic development dynamics. A good part of its tertialisation is being achieved by speculative financial transactions with their inherently greater risks and uncertainties than in the industrial countries. Such dangers have been demonstrated by Mexico's peso crisis and its repercussions on the whole of Latin America.

In some Third World countries, a "location annuity" has replaced the old raw materials one. Here it's about providing locations for off-shore transactions which offer international capital traders a maximum of freedom of movement combined with low taxation. Suitable for such operations are small countries which, despite low levy rates, achieve significant income in macroeconomic terms.

The radical changes in the world economy are spurring the differentiation of the Third World Without, however, necessarily fostering a dissolution of the Third World as an "imaginary community". It is precisely the advanced countries of East and South-East Asia that are showing a certain interest in the formulation of joint positions of the "South" in order to secure their own positional gains in the global economy. It's not by chance that the non-aligned countries and the Group of 77 have formed a joint coordination committee, and that the ASEAN countries are changing course on the international human rights policy.

Hitherto, the developing countries' strategy was to broaden the concept of human rights as a justification for demands on the industrial nations. But of late some developing countries, led by the ASEAN states, have questioned the universal validity of human rights even after their universality was confirmed by consensus at the Conference on Human Rights in Vienna in 1993. Playing a role in this policy is the governments' fear that due to the expansion of global communications networks, the behaviour patterns and preferences of their own people could in some way become similar to those of the West. As the rulers see it, that would be detrimental to the continuation of the development models practised so far.

Internet Creates New Cultural Dimension

Much information which Asian governments view as subversive in already globally available on the Internet. The old struggle over the world information order, which at first was primarily a clinch between East and West, is thus taking on a new dimension. For with the growing importance of computer literacy to a country's ability to assert itself on world markets, the Asian threshold countries have not only an interest in controlling the on-line communication but also to expand it and the know-how that it requires.

Even the critics of any interventions in the internet and other global communications networks must admit that modern communications technologies are politically blind and their use in itself does not represent progress. The setting up and expansion of global information highways will offer forum not only to people who want to use it for education and enlightenment, but also to all shades of fundamentalists. These highways will not necessarily bring the misery of many Third World regions closer to the industrial countries, but possibly rather strengthen the tendency to process all world events as entertainment.

Global Two-thirds Society

The gravest aspect of the current upheaval in the world economy is its negative impact on jobs. The information economy needs for fewer workers than an economy based on materials. Instead, the demands on the skills of the workers are growing. Twenty per cent of the world workforce will in future be employed as (overworked) "intelligence workers". Eighty per cent will work part–time, if they are not underemployed or jobless. So the tertialisation of the global economy delivers more underemployment rather than more leisure time. The workers who are rationalised out of their jobs in the industrial sector cannot be absorbed by the service sector because it, too, is not left untouched by rationalisation measures. The civil service is also cutting back on staff. At all levels, there's a race to make the greatest possible savings on payrolls. At the same time, there's growing pressure to cut costs in providing for the victims of this development. That means thinning out the social security safety net.

The bottom line is that the two-thirds society, which developmental action groups hitherto assumed was limited to the Third World, is spreading worldwide. That, however, will not in the foreseeable future lead to an amendment of the North-South disparities. It's true that the change in the global economy is taking place faster, and to a greater extent in the industrial nations. But rationalisation is also happening in the developing countries in a bid to boost their competitiveness. So the upheaval in the world economy aggravates the problems which exist in a majority of the developing countries, while creating new ones in the industrial nations. The need for action on the North-South policy is growing, while the industrial nations. The need for action on the North-South Policy is growing, while the industrial nations' scope for concessions and compromises is shrinking. The new social question which is now crystallizing at global level is not being answered. The consequences are unforeseeable.

Another Loser?

It's more probable that a sharpening of the North–South confrontation is to be reckoned with. For the industrial nations will attempt to keep the social costs of the information economy at bay for as long as possible. The trade unions will thereby compete with the developing countries for jobs for their members. But this policy has its limits precisely because of the peaking of the problems in the industrial nations. Overstepping these limits means war, and passively accepting them chaos and social decay. Solutions could be sought in two directions: effective taxation of the information economies, and the creation of jobs in the non-profit sector. But it's possible there are no global solutions for global problems. That would mean for at least part of the Third World a renewal of the old debate on partial decoupling from the world economy.

18

Lightening the Load for Women

Not only do women in India suffer greater poverty than men, they often have little choice but to pass it on to the next generation. Investing in women, therefore, is an effective way of building a better economic future for the poor.

Research findings from all sources are confirming what development practitioners have long observed: women are generally worse off economically than men, and the consequences of their poverty are more serious for future generations.

Women's poverty differs from that of men both in degree and in kind: women experience greater poverty and transmit their disadvantage more readily to their children, thus perpetuating the poverty cycle. At the same time, however, they are better able than men to protect children from the consequences of poverty.

It is this close connection between women's and children's fortunes that makes women's poverty a prime target for enlightened development practice. Anti-poverty policies need to reach poor women both to maximise social return on development investments and minimise the poverty of this and the next generation.

Breaking the Poverty Cycle

Poor women's rising participation in the world of paid work, however, does not necessarily guarantee a destiny of poverty. On the contrary, their earnings can protect children from poverty. Until fairly recently, the prevailing assumption was that any positive income effect of women's employment on children's health and well-being would be offset by negative effects of reduced childcare time by working mothers or by the substitution of older siblings in childcare. Recent studies, however, indicate a positive effect of women's employment on child health and nutrition. Women prefer to invest meagre earnings on child well-being and underscore the point that the income poor women earn can yield higher social benefits than income earned by men.

These positive effects of poor women's income-earning activities are not necessarily contradictory with the negative effects of women's increased work on their daughter's educational opportunities. It is likely that women need a minimum level of income to act on their preference to invest scarce resources on child well-being, below which their additional work perpetuates rather than halts poverty.

Policy and Research Implications

It is therefore desirable to implement policies that reinforce the virtuous cycle between women's and children's well-being that can occur in poor families when women have more income, and avoid those that can instead trigger a vicious cycle of deprivation between mothers and children. Circumstances which increase poor women's unpaid or very low-paid work can foster the perpetuation of disadvantage. These include the effects of declining household incomes during economic downturns, the decrease in service provision by the State which accompanies structural adjustment programmes, and many community and child-centred interventions that rely heavily on women's unpaid time. Anti-poverty packages need to reinforce poor women's roles as economic producers and avoid actions which increase women's unpaid labour for the promotion of family child welfare.

Projects which increase women's productivity in home and market production and expand their employment options can help turn the vicious cycle of poverty into a virtuous one. This necessitates executing agencies, which can work with women, in budget allocations to strengthen the capacity of institutions to implement and monitor gender-responsive employment programmes for the poor.

The reach of project interventions is restricted, however. Their impact is often short-lived and while they can help to contain the cycle of poverty between mothers and children, they cannot in themselves transform women's economic activities. Changes in the policy environment are required for the latter. These include agricultural policies which target poor farmer and give women farmers access to land, credit and technical assistance; financial policies which promote the growth of small enterprises and foster entrepreneurship among women; and labour-intensive "pro-poor" economic growth policies. In addition, governments need to invest in upgrading women's occupational skills, and in a series of complementary measures, including overhauling social security systems, establishing gender-friendly regulatory frameworks for agricultural and industrial growth, and legislate on childcare options.

To guide these policies, we need: research that distinguishes families from households and seeks to understand the formation, structure and dynamics of families headed by women; longitudinal studies which provide a narrative for events in women's lives and assess the transmission of disadvantage between mothers and children; trend data which tracks changes in women's work as a result of changes in economic conditions and in implementation of economic and social policies; and, analyses of the mechanics, costs and consequences of targeting interventions to female heads of households and poor women.

The policy-oriented research agenda is perhaps as ambitious as the policy agenda and both require funding. Investing in women should be an effective use of scarce development resources if these actions are guided by the basic principle of seeing women in India for what they are economic and social agents and not merely passive recipients of welfare.

19

Women in Politics

Breaking Through the Barriers

The participation of women in political life is today on the agendas of most political parties in India. However, attempts to translate this goal into concrete reality have had limited success. A basic reason for this is the lack of conceptual clarity about the genuine commitment to the issue. For any such endeavour to be successful, it must be recognised that the equal participation of women and men in decision-making in all spheres is a prerequisite for effective democracy.

Participation means more than female membership in political parties, female voter turnout in elections or a token female presence in political bodies. Participation must be meaningful and effective, and must include representation in the political arena. This includes not only formal or higher level decision-making forums, but also other political units: the family, community groups, associations, trade unions and local bodies. These are crucial areas for intervention within which women can easily understand the issues and play an effective role.

The identification of barriers to women's political participation is obviously a prerequisite for overcoming them, but the visible barriers do not necessarily reflect the entire situation, and are often merely indicative of more deep-rooted problems. Governments tend to address the issue by devising measures capable of showing quick results. But tackling visible barriers without addressing their root causes results at best in temporary success.

Overcoming the barriers means not only eliminating them but also ensuring women's participation through other means. Affirmative action measures should not be perceived as privileges or concessions, but as interim measures to reverse existing imbalances, until such time as genuine equality and parity is achieved.

India must review its policies, constitution and legislation to see whether these have been discriminatory towards women, or have been ineffective in promoting women's rights. Since the issue of women's participation cannot be addressed in isolation, one must identify and assess factors affecting the development of a democratic culture or the recognition of human rights concerns. These factors include the country's political history, its socio-cultural, ethnic and religious diversity, the impact of traditional, customary, feudal and tribal laws, and the use of religious interpretations regarding women's rights.

One must review the prevalent general situation of women. While inequalities and imbalances exist in all places, some have stronger patriarchal structures wherein gender roles are more rigidly assigned. It is particularly important to assess women's political participation, including political rights, participation in election process and political parties, representation in legislative bodies and local councils, women in the civil service and in trade unions, and women's groups and lobbies.

Barriers to women's political participation can be legal, social, financial or political. In addition to identifying such barriers, it is useful to assess initiatives taken by governments and non-governmental organisations (NGOs), to evaluate successes and failures, identify the reasons and make modifications.

Based on the above, appropriate multi-pronged strategies and actions must be devised. It is important to develop a clear policy articulating the effective involving of women in the formulation of laws and policies which govern their lives.

Measures must be taken to ensure the principle of equality as a fundamental right. National legislation must be amended or repealed to remove any discriminatory provision. Positive legislation must be introduced to promote or protect affirmative action measures. The language of the law must clearly address itself to men and women, changing the practice of using the legal 'he' to include 'she'.

Research must be undertaken to cover information gaps. Monitoring mechanisms, guidelines and indicators must be devised and a process of periodic data collection established to assess changing trends. Documentation and analysis of innovative initiatives must be ongoing, to help in devising and modifying strategies.

Women's human rights and power sharing issues must be integrated in all training programmes of government, semi-government and autonomous institutions. Key personnel involved in decision-making and implementation need to be made sensitive to gender issues. Political education and training programmes for women are needed at the community level, for NGOs and community-based organisations, communicators, development workers and media personnel, etc.

Campaigns to change attitudes and social norms and project a positive image of women can be run through educational efforts and the media, and public discussions and debates. A clear stand should be taken against any misrepresentation of religion which stands in the way of women's equality and political participation.

Workshops and seminars should promote closer interaction between women in NGOs, advocacy and research groups, government departments, political leadership, trade unions, worker's associations and the media.

A minimum quota should be established for women in all sectors and grades of the civil service, including government, semi-government and autonomous organisations. A minimum percentage of key advisory positions, directorships, etc. should be reserved for women. Advertisements for government jobs should specifically state women's eligibility.

Electoral rolls should be systematically updated to include all eligible women. Education should be provided on electoral rights, political parties, election issues and concrete ways of holding candidates and political parties accountable. Political parties should publish their positions on women's rights issues, and encourage women to vote on issues that concern them. Constitutions of political parties should exclude provisions which condone or justify discrimination.

An adequate minimum representation of women in legislative bodies and local councils can be ensured by reserving seats through such means as putting women's names in priority positions on lists, providing financial support to female candidates, and making legal provisions that only those parties which give certain minimum number of tickets to women are eligible to contest elections.

A government ministry with the requisite authority should be designated as a focal point for devising policy, ensuring implementation and coordinating with other ministries and agencies.

An autonomous Permanent Commission on the Status of Women should be set up to function as a thinktank on women's issues, to commission policy research and to review, recommend and monitor the implementation of policies and programmes in the field of development, rights and political participation. The Commission should comprise government representatives, NGOs, human rights organisations and experts in different areas.

A judicial authority should expedite women's human rights cases; this could take the form of a human rights bench, a tribunal or an equality ombudsman. These are only some of the basic principles and guidelines that can be adopted. Ultimately, however, no strategy can be effective unless it is also backed by the requisite political will and impetus.

20

Consuming the Future

Now that we are to reach six billion of us, it is a good point to check again on what sort of lifestyles we pursue and what is the environmental impact of those lifestyles. It is curious that we have spent several decades being concerned about the growing numbers of humankind while not giving at least an equal amount of attention to the levels of living we aspire to, and how many natural resources we chew up thereby and how much pollution and waste we cause.

Everybody is a consumer of sorts. True, every fifth person scarcely qualifies for that designation, consuming goods worth less than $1 per day. Conversely, every seventh person qualifies for a designation of super-consumer, with a cash income at least fifty times greater. These latter are the people who, through their carbon dioxide emissions, are disrupting everybody's climate dozens of times more than the average citizen of One Earth. Fair Play, anyone?

Much as the have-nots seek to match the have's, it is plain their efforts will not work out for a long time to come, at best. If every Chinese person were to consume just one additional chicken per year and if the said chicken were to be raised primarily on grain, this would account for as much grain per year as all the grain exports of the number two exporter, Canada. If the Chinese were to raise their per-capita consumption of beef, now only 4 kgs per year, to that of Americans, 45 kg, and if the additional beef were produced largely in feedlots after the manner of the United

States, it would account for as much extra grain as the entire US grain harvest, less than one-third of which is exported. Because of its recent climbing up the food chain toward a meat-based diet, China has become one of the world's leading importers of grain. The global grain market today is around 200 million tons per year, and shows scant scope for significant increase.

As a further measure of its ambitions, the Chinese government has designated the auto industry as one of five industry "pillars". Today China has fewer cars than Los Angeles. If per-capita car ownership, together with oil consumption, were to match that of the United States, China would need 80 million barrels of oil per day—by contrast with the world's 1996 oil output of 64 million barrels of oil per day. The surge in carbon dioxide emissions would be unprecedented.

All this notwithstanding, there are already some 250 million newly affluent people in China. They are people with a household income equivalent to perhaps US$20,000, and enough discretionary income to enjoy the perquisites of the good life as perceived by these nouveaux riches. Top of the shopping lists are meat and more meat, followed by cars whether big or small. These are the badges of success: they show you have arrived.

The new consumers in China are matched by at least 200 million in India, and tens of millions in South Korea, Taiwan, Malaysia and Thailand (the recent economic setbacks have not permanently punctured the economic bubbles). Then there are 200 million more in Brazil, Argentina, Venezuela and Mexico, and more again in Hungary and other countries of Eastern Europe, also Turkey. Put them all together and they total about as many as the 800 million long established consumers in the ultra rich countries (the OECD grouping). When the current economic hiccups in Asia are left behind, the ranks of the new consumers can be expected to rise rapidly.

But they cannot hope to become super consumers. Where would all the extra gain come from? How could the global climate tolerate the huge additional pulse of carbon dioxide? There are all kinds of other environmental reasons to suppose that environmental constraints will become all the more constraining. True, technology could help moderate the environmental impact. We could enjoy twice as much material prosperity while using only half as much natural resources and causing half as much pollution and waste. But the new consumers will want to pursue the American dream to the hilt, and it is hard to see that the best technologies could enable huge numbers of affluent aspirants, perhaps two billion people by 2010, enjoying even half the material prosperity of Americans with average household incomes of $40,000.

But is it true "prosperity"—mental and emotional as well as material? Or is the American dream becoming a nightmare with its harried lifestyles and declining leisure time, where the shopping mall is the ultimate Mecca, and the good life is a case of piling up goodies?

In any case, we cannot expect the new consumers to forego their "rightful share" of affluence unless the long-time affluent agree to cut back on their environmental ruinous lifestyles. It is these communities that must offer a strong example, and soonest. Where is the political leader who will espouse the new vision, however much it may be perceived as the ultimate vote loser?

Health Care Relief in Conflict Situations

What Can We Learn from the Food Relief Experience?

Conflicts and war occur in many of the poorest nations where populations already suffer from severe ill health. War leads to an increase in disease and to a worsening of the already fragile condition of populations. Health care itself becomes a victim of conflict. Many deaths which occur during these emergencies are not discretely related to the conflict itself but are the result of lacking access to public health services. Furthermore, conflict itself but are the result of lacking access to public health services. Furthermore, conflict contributes to the deterioration of already pre-existing structural weaknesses of the health care system. An example is the period of internal conflict in Uganda (1970-1986) when health services declined in the aftermath of the war due to the impact of foreign assistance and the planning vacuum in which the activities took place.

The Impact of Conflict on Health Care

Conflict and civil strife may lead to a major disruption of health services. This is not only a result of physical destruction but also of finding shortages since national governments increase spending on military activities. Casualties increase the demand for curative services, which can divert already limited resources from preventive care.

In the case of the Sudanese civil war a large majority of health professionals was forced to abandon rural health professionals was forced to abandon rural health services and left for urban areas or neighbouring countries in order to find new employment. Entire preventive health services such as immunisation as well as water and sanitation projects collapsed leaving the population exposed to infectious diseases and epidemics. In urban areas, the gap in public health care provision is sometimes filled with the expansion of private services. In rural areas, private sector involvement in health care is rather marginal, apart from some omission hospitals or pharmacies. Therefore the non-formal health care sector often makes a substantial contribution towards health care.

With the rise internal conflicts in Africa, more people suffer from emergency situations. This also increases the influence and impact of international donors. External assistance nowadays accounts for more than 25 per cent of government health expenditure in Sub-Saharan Africa.

The size of donor involvement reflects the power of international agencies to control the policy domain. Countries in conflict or post-conflict situations are under pressure to 'rescue' their health systems and accept global policies in exchange for aid assistance and relief.

However, in the period after 1991, donor organisations tended to increase their expenditures for high profile humanitarian operations rather than ordinary development activities. This shift may reflect the increasing influence of media covering some of the conflicts. Too often, organisations intervene with ad hoc assistance without sufficient consultation at local level.

Donors' Perceptions in Designing Relief Interventions

Today, in many parts of Sub-Saharan Africa development assistance has virtually collapsed and has been substituted by relief assistance. The problem is that relief interventions are based on a Western construction of reality, reflecting what is desirable and necessary in times of conflict. Most interventions therefore stress physical and material needs, presuming that the social aspect of food and health is not an immediate issue to address.

The question which arises here is on who's views and perceptions these needs are based? While donors interest may be guided from the perspective of ill-health, the recipient government may be concerned with the collapse of the economy. However, any intervention needs to take into account that local knowledge and practices are shaped by state interests as well as power relationships. The common belief that health care systems always collapse due to conflict is sometimes mistaken, considering the fact that today's internal conflicts are often fragmented, conflicts do not necessarily result in a breakdown of the health care delivery system.

Donors tend to respond with a 'package approach and developing countries ministries of health increasingly play a symbolic role. The evidence suggests that international organisation tend to create vertical programmes, which undermine national public health programmes. Foreign interventions are technically sophisticated and reorienting health are towards a more curative approach. Too little attention given to strengthen the health care system within its own limits, providing more appropriate technology, drugs and emphasizing the training of local health staff.

Another vital issue concerns the existence of already fragile health information systems. Agencies tend to bring their own systems which leads to further fragmentation. The local perspective on what are the 'basic needs' in physical and social health are usually not considered. Health relief interventions do not recognize the potential of the communities and the non-formal health sector such as healers and traditional midwifes in supporting and maintaining health care sector presents a substantial contribution towards health. It is not the question between choosing either allopathic or traditional services, it is more the decision which kind of illness will be best treated by which practitioner. There is a need in further exploring the role of this sector particularly since this is sometimes the only service available for certain populations.

Responding to Local Needs

More community-based public health interventions could be vital to reduce mortality and morbidity. For example in Somalia during the 1992 war and famine high mortality rates due to measles and diarrhoea could have been prevented by involving the communities in primary health care activities such as immunisation and nutrition improvement.

In the African context Tigray is an example where health services had been sustained and partially expanded during the civil war against the Ethiopian government. Local government structures called baitos promoting social and economic development. Baitos encouraged communities to establish revolving funds for drugs and medical equipment. It actually functioned as early type of community financing system.

As mentioned above, the challenge in changing health care relief strategies is to overcome the approach of short-term interventions, particularly in changing conflict environment where conflicts are complex and interruptions are no longer short-term.

Therefore interventions need to be linked with the process of conflict resolution to avoid health care or food aid being used by politically dominant groups.

Food Relief in Conflict Situations

Food interventions have both a survival and a production function. For example, food-for-work may be part of an income programme or food aid can be magnetised to generate local currency. However, food aids have to be seen beyond the objective to fulfil nutritional goals, it also defines relationships between social groups in regard to food accessibility and how food is shared. Food aid is aiming to meet people's basic food requirements and minimising risk and severity of disease by complementing services such as basic health care.

In more stable political conditions where free food aid is given it presents an income transfer by releasing income, which normally is spent on food. However, in conflict situations food relief frequently becomes part of the dynamics of conflict such in the case of Sudan where it is used to sustain the struggle between the North and the South without resolving it. Furthermore, the military attack food supplies in the fight against rebels who depend on the support from the communities.

Health is also a matter of food security. When food insecurity coincides with conflict situations, health and survival are threatened. Food security provided some concepts on how and why vulnerable households manage to survive in periods of hardship (coping strategies).

Coping Strategies in African Trouble Zones

Today, most conflicts in Africa such as the ones in the Great Lake Region, Angola or Congo cause major problems of food insecurity. They are linked to the civil wars which produce substantial social disruption as a result of massive population movements. The analysis of coping strategies showed that household respond to these conflict situation by eating less, selling livestock and land, or trying to find new sources of income.

In some emergency situations, however such coping mechanisms may fall. In the case of the war in Mozambique food aid was vital since coping strategies were limited and people had to sell all their assets, which was particular, true for internationally displaced persons and refugees.

It has been argued that food relief bypasses local structures in favour of those qualifying on a nutrition status criterion, decided by international organisation, or it may attract populations to refugee camps to receive free food rations and thereby undermines local production. In the case of Rwanda food aid was targeted at the internally displaced and left out the local population. This can be due to donor bias in needs assessment.

Food scarcity is not always so result of civil war but its creation may be rather a political objective. An example is food relief manipulated by local elites and the military like in the case of Sudan. It can be summarised that generally relief operations often bear the risk of fueling the process of instability and violence rather than helping to contain the situation.

Lessons from Food Relief for the Health Sector?

Through the experience of food relief in recent civil wars such as Sudan, Somalia, Mozambique etc., there has been an increasing awareness of the economic and political context in which operations takes place. Like food relief, health care is a political tool, which can, if not properly targeted, undermine peoples access to health care services. While food production is linked to food security, it is more difficult to identify factors leading to self-sufficiency in health care.

As mentioned above, food aid is aiming to insure survival. It also has an economic aspect, protecting household assets. Health care relief is targeted to assure immediate physical survival based on the importance of social health. Unfortunately, curative interventions hardly consider the socio-cultural dimension of health. Therefore it would be beneficial if health care interventions consider local norms and traditions. Interventions should be compatible and complement local health programmes. The emphasis should be on strengthening formal and non-formal health institutions both in service provision and training.

In food relief, distribution and needs assessment identification are controversial issues for discussion. While the programme design is shaped by donor's perceptions, the actual programmes are influenced by the priorities of some powerful leaders as well as the socio-economic and political context.

Health care interventions need to analyse these issues in the context of economic and political systems in order to identify the most vulnerable groups, for example populations living in areas which are more, operations require a stronger involvement of communities both as users and active participants carry out and maintain public health programmes.

There is a need for a new concept to be designed, which applies, to chronic emergencies. In the absence of a policy framework, guidelines need to be developed in order to overcome the inconsistency in planning and implementation. Donors need to change their assumptions on which they plan their health relief responses. A starting point in improving the efficiency of these operations is to provide institutional support to local authorities and organisations and involve them in the planning and implementation of programmes.

22

No Progress Without a Secular Society

Every day, women continue to be victims of rape, trafficking, acid-throwing, dowry deaths and other kinds of torture. At the opening of this new century, women are still not considered as equal human beings in many parts of the world. Religion and patriarchy continue to have an all-encroaching hold on their lives, maintaining and justifying their age-old oppression. In some South Asian Societies, this hold is even increasing.

I do not believe that there can be real equality in a society dominated by religion. Western countries speak repeatedly about the necessity of economic development to alleviate poverty. But this is not enough. Some oil rich countries may be economically developed, but women are deprived of all rights. The supremacy of religion is incompatible with freedom of expression, women's rights and democracy. This is why I see religion as the main enemy of women's development.

We have to act on several fronts at once. First of all, improving access to education. In a society like Bangladesh, 80 per cent of women are illiterate. For centuries women have been taught they are the slaves of men. It is very hard to change their minds, to make them aware of their oppression, to give them a sense of their independence. This educational effort has to go hand in hand with a secular feminist movement in society. Such movements have to start within the country and they cannot take hold when people are uneducated and unaware of their oppression. I'm not sure you can accomplish much from the outside, except to expose in the media the atrocities women in all too many countries face in their day to day lives.

In some countries, this movement is emerging, but very timidly, and it has a slim margin of maneuver. It has the uphill task of fighting for the repeal of religious laws and the introduction of a uniform civil code. So far, it tends to be constituted by a few individual feminists who are forced to be diplomatic, to compromise with fundamentalists, be they men or women. But they are trying to change the system, step by step, and it will take a very long time. People are not yet ready to do away with religious laws that impact upon every aspect of society, from education and health to the workplace and the home.

For women's status to change, we also need enlightened leaders who believe in equality. In countries of South Asia women with a strong voice do not have the support of political leaders, whether they be men or women. Look at the countries in which women are in politics, or even heads of state. Does it follow that women in those countries are emancipated? Because of long-standing vested interests such leaders continue to back measures that oppress women. They are not ideologically committed to changing these conditions. In South Asia, most of the women who become heads of state are religious, and like men, they adhere to the religious objectives of the establishment.

Until a society is not based on religion and women are considered equal to men before the law, I do not think that politics will advance the cause of women. In Western countries, women are educated, they are treated equally, they have access to jobs. In these conditions, their participation in politics has a meaning.

Education, a secular feminist movement, and leaders—both men and women—committed to equality and justice. This is what it will take to change the dire conditions which too many women still face today. It will take a very long time, but we are here to work towards that end.

23

What was Wrong with Structural Adjustment

In Defence of a Much-Maligned Strategy

After decades of stranded development theories, ideologies and paradigms, "structural adjustment", with its demands for clean fiscal policy and an end to uneconomic state enterprises, political privileges, market and exchange rate intervention and corruption, entered the aid arena like a refreshing dawn after a long night of frustrating dreams. Only the "old guard" of planned economy advocates and jealous academicians who had missed the boat were able to shut their eyes to the moral and economic justification of this liberating breakthrough international development policy spearheaded by the Breton Woods institutions then steered by some exceptionally courageous economists.

Reaction to SAPs

As with any revolution, defeat is awaiting the pioneers at the hands of political power greed, reactionary tactics by the formerly privileged and academic envy. The principal device serving the reactionary forces as a lever of influence on the mood of the "development community" has been the identification and dramatisation of new pockets or strata of (principally urban) poverty allegedly created by structural adjustment measures, while shunning the much broader-based rise in economic activity, real incomes and sense of fair reward in the overall society, especially the rural population. That the hardship experienced by urban poor, formerly privileged under consumer price control and import subsidies to the debit depressed farm prices or maintained by grossly over expanded public payrolls, was only laying open the camouflaged erosion of the economy and near-bankruptcy of governments and public enterprises, was conveniently downplayed.

These reactionary howls were to be expected. Not that they met the entirely innocent. There had been naively sweeping, overly assuming demands by some structural adjustment missions. But an intellectually vigorous and dynamic "development community" would have coped with the ensuing opposition, strengthened the analytical and monitoring capacities and the political will to endure also rocky roads and bitter medicines on the way to a healthier base. Instead institutional rivalry, political opportunism and emotive populism were thriving. In a way, the "development community" behaved as if it did not want its patient to become able to stand on his own feet and eventually steal its raison d'être.

Worst, the Bretton Woods Institutions themselves, partly under the pressure of the emotive opposition described above fell to the temptation to rescue their lending volume, which was threatened by the frugality dictated to Third World public budgets under structural adjustment recipes, through hardship-easing loans. They thereby corrupted their creation in using it to reinforce their indispensability. As a consequence it soon turned out that some of the most obedient loan takers under structural adjustment terms experienced sharply rising indebtedness, exploited as a disqualifying symptom by the anti-structural adjustment camp.

Whatever the opinions on structural adjustment policies, the commitment to the principles of "good governance" has come to stay, at least on paper, as an almost standard conditionally for official development aid from OECD donor countries. The realisation, matured in the implementation of structural adjustment programmes, that not the quantity of aid, but the quality of Third World government determines the positive or negative course of development, may be regarded as the most valuable fruit of the decades-old-policy debate in the 'development community". And the use of aid a pressure or bribing factor towards "good governance" as foreign aid's least disputable purpose.

Out of the Limelight

Nothing, however, must be taken for granted. Achievement breeds its challenge! Structural adjustment, though in essence hardly disputable has been pushed out of the limelight and replaced by the oldest actor in the company, eradication of poverty, twinned with an equally perpetual endeavour at the macro-level: debt-forgiveness. This falling back to square one in donors approach to the problems of the south, i.e., the call to alleviate poverty and priorities direct efforts to this end above all other developmental efforts—does it indicate a sell-out of constructive ideas in the "development community"? Has any noteworthy progress been achieved in the past by this approach?

By telling a frugally toiling but independent subsistence farmer that internationally his condition is classed as "poverty", deserving compassion and support by the world community and cancellation of his debts, one can hardly expect a sustainable improvement in his output, satisfaction, or self-respect and even less, when he realises that the help principally provides jobs, fringe benefits and self-importance to a gamut of intermediaries, at home and abroad.

What do those poverty advocates (the "Lords of poverty") really know about the resources, life managements, value systems and ambitions of those they generalize by the billions? The great variance in the conception of life situations, from different external viewpoints.

What the aid system can do for these rural populations classed as "poor"/"underprivileged"/"exploited", is press for justice, i.e., "good governance". The achievement of structural adjustment policy through e.g. abolishing official price and exchange rate distortions, import subsidies and exploitative state agencies, has brought massive income improvement for peasant populations, i.e. the majority of LDC inhabitants, in dimensions unreachable by whatsoever direct "attack" on rural "poverty". What people want is not being benevolently treated as poor, but being justly rewarded for their work, i.e., by access to the unmanipulated market of their output. Slackening on structural adjustment/"good governance" conditionally under the present "10 year itch" for paradigm change means foregoing much of the potential opportunities for undoing injustice and exploitation of the masses. It should be clear where priority focus should be placed in ODA policy.

Small is Not Beautiful

The direct attack on "poverty", orchestrated by the Bretton Woods institutions under their freshly launched Poverty Reduction Strategy Paper (PRSP) campaign, is being rightly regarded as primarily an NGO domain, since most activities are expected to be carried out at local community level. This would require careful screening and coordinating of NGO activities and their integration via gradual expansion of their experience. But "small" is not "beautiful" for the development financing institutions. Disbursement needs are pressing, calling for the new paradigm to quickly provide channels for another wave of loans to the "IDA Countries". Their problem of heavy indebtedness, which would principally exclude most of them from any new loan consideration, shall be solved with one stroke (which only the well-cushioned development bureaucracy can afford); debt relief against presentation of country PRSPs by the respective governments. NGOs are expected of play in the system especially the knowledge gap about the "poor" people's real wants and needs NGOs will naturally be tempted by such expansionary boost to their involvement (referred to sarcastically as their philanthropic empire" by an African conference participant), but this will not be conducive to quality and accountability of their performance, which ideally should be based on private sponsorship in combination with strong target-group provided self-help components.

Patience and Self-Restraint

Local knowledge and initiatives cannot be obtained under time pressure. "The grass does not grow faster by being pulled". When will the "development community" learn patience and self-restraint in the approach to LDC's capacity for constructive absorption of aid programmes accompanied by a genuine sense of ownership?

After all these deliberations, how shall development policy be shaped in order to better correspond with reality, without sinking deeper into hypocrisy and frustration?

To come back to the opening question: what was wrong with "structural adjustment"? Nothing was wrong with its intent. In fact this was very right and long overdue. Its implementation, however, lacked patience, perseverance and solid support from the development community, apart from its being corrupted as a vehicle for expansionary lending policy. If aid is meant to not be an end in itself, then structural adjustment policy needs constant reinforcement, underpinned by strict lending discipline. There should be an end to irresponsible lending and easy escape from its consequences by wholesome periodic debt relief burdened on the international tax-paying community. No ODA, either loans or grants, should be made available to governments who are not in active process of implementing "good governance" principles. A monitoring unit, reporting to the donor community on government performance in regard to its "-good government"? Structural adjustment commitment, should be maintained in each and receiving country by "donor consortia" comprising all locally represented bilateral and multilateral development organisations currently extending technical, financial or material assistance to the country.

In order to accommodate the poverty focus without diluting the necessary structural adjustment orientation of ODA, a division of activity-focus between the latter and the NGO sector would seem to be advantageous.

- ODA, limited to the countries abiding to structural adjustment/"good governance" conditionally, with focus concentration on sustainable physical, social and economic infrastructure principally at national and regional level, public management training, higher education and research, consultant and senior adviser services.

- The NGO sector, principally funded by private sponsorship, united to structural adjustment conditionally (but preferably grafted on local self-help initiative), with focus-concentration on the "Third World "poor", i.e. mostly at rural community and low-income township level, for amelioration of living conditions and local resource utilisation.

- Strengthening of linkages between the NGO sector and the UN Technical Agencies to mutual benefit: NGOs in need of professional information, evaluation and advice, of forum for discussion to find an actively supportive window at the agencies; the latter to maintain and develop field contact for research and policy generation, not least as a substitute for their declining project work (giving way to greater concentration on their global functions i.e., serving as information, policy initiation, and coordination/ negotiation centre on topics of global concern, such as e.g.: human rights, global monetary and trade systems, tropical forest and global marine resources, global and regional health threats, international standards).

In conclusion, it may be called to mind that aid and its institutions have no claim for permanence. They are justified only as temporary functions in a phasing-out process of self-help support. Any claim for unlimited continuity would breed lasting infantilisation.

24

Development

The People Know Best

Meetings of the World Bank and the World Trade Organisation has inspired high-mined protest and, on occasion, even vandalism. But this protest and vandalism may miss the point. It is hard to blame those who complain of bullying or blundering by the great institutions of global power. But the poor of the world, especially the poor of developing countries, deserve more than street demonstrations. The poor understand better than anybody the complicated details of their own poverty – the absence of health care, the lack of education, and all the sinister perils to their own safety and well-being. They know the failures of their governments, and of international institutions.

And that is the point: It is the people of the poor countries who will have to apply new knowledge to design and achieve their own development. A country can only develop when its citizens have the freedom to address their own development problems. The obligation of the rich countries, is to give help where they can. And anyone who doesn't see a moral imperative to contribute to a fairer, more prosperous future is free to frame the obligation differently—as self-interest, for example. It will surely serve us better to invest in a peaceful and contented global community than to invite the strife and poverty of unanswered injustice and economic ruin.

Among our relevant conclusions: Powerful institutions of global finance and trade (not least, the World Bank and the World Trade Organisation) can be a source of real promise to poor countries. If governed right, they can help integrate developing economies into the enriching opportunities of global trade and investment. But such promise is often wasted because the very poverty of poor-country governments weakens their ability to negotiate the terms that would serve them best.

Communities in poor countries find themselves at a special disadvantage when it comes to bargaining with foreign investors. Investment can bring growth and spread wealth. It can also threaten human rights and social cohesion, or cultural integrity, and the fragile balance of ecosystems. Nobel economist Amartya Sen has spoken powerfully about the intimate relation between development and choice, the subject of his thought-provoking book Development as Freedom. Development, Sen argues, "consists of the removal of various types of unfreedoms that leave people with little choice and little opportunity..." He defines freedom as "both the primary end and the principal means of development."

A precondition of this freedom is knowledge—knowledge of the hard facts and the hard science on which real choices are constructed, also it is knowledge of good governance—procedures of choice that are effective, responsive and democratic. For budgetary reasons, rich countries contribution in international development was severely cut in the 1990s. Now, along with others in the rich countries, they have to begin to reinvest in international development.

This means a new commitment to the improvement of lives, and to the future that the North must share with the South. It will be a reinvestment in peace, and in our own prosperity. This remains a matter of obligation, and of sensible self-interest.

25

Can Economic Growth Reduce Poverty?

New Findings on Inequality, Economic Growth and Poverty

Many people still think first of 'economic growth' in relation to poverty reduction. Indeed, their correlation is one of the most-discussed issues of combating poverty. The relationship is of great importance because if there is a clear causal dependency, reducing poverty could fundamentally be limited to measures to promote growth. However, if there was low growth or stagnation it would not be possible to reduce poverty decisively. In the opposite case, that of the phenomena having no causal relation, promising measures to reduce poverty could be taken up even without economic growth.

Hardly anyone now explicitly expresses the view that economic development trickles down automatically to the poor. Practical experience has refuted this assumption dating from the early days of development policy in the 1960s. However, a number of studies show development of growth and a decline in poverty running parallel. On the other hand, there are also examples which show that despite high economic growth, poverty is not reduced markedly. The common answer to the question this raises is thus: Yes, growth can reduce poverty, but only if additional measures oriented on the poor are taken up. This is often termed pro-poor-growth. But what that means in detail, and whether economic growth as such plays a causal role at all, is not clarified. It is worth taking a look at the arguments on the basis of more recent empirical and theoretical knowledge.

No Direct Causality Between Growth and Poverty Reduction

Among the many indicators of poverty, the income of the poor (income poverty) has the closest relationship to economic growth. An increase in gross domestic product and thus national income could, if other factors come into play be linked with an increase in the per capita income of the poor.

Such a relationship between economic growth and the income of the poor, however, cannot be described as causal, as is asserted implicitly time and again by the statement that growth is a necessary but not sufficient precondition for poverty reduction. In so far as growth and poverty reduction arise at the same time at the end of a process, they exist alongside each other. It would be almost a tautology to say that the former is the cause or part-cause of the latter. Both express the same thing, namely a change in per capita income as well, and both have similar causes. What matters is recognising what these causes are and what specific factors must come into play so that the income of the poor grows too. Growth as a "prerequisite" or "condition" is then no longer the focus; the priority is asking for specific policies that result in higher incomes for the poor. The detour in thinking about growth is not necessary. Since, however, it is based on similar factors, such as fiscal policy/budget structure, employment policy, combating inflation, and institutional development, economic growth can also emerge if poverty is reduced. The difference of views lies in the fact that under the heading 'poverty reduction' the aim is no longer growth, but a purposeful reduction of poverty.

Therefore, in reverse, successful combating of poverty can be seen as being the cause of growth insofar as activating the capabilities of the poor and using their productive capacity of the poor and using their productive capacity triggers economic drive.

Indirect Causality Between Growth and Poverty Reduction?

So even if economic growth fundamentally has no direct causal impact on poverty, growth still can reduce it indirectly. This is the case when due to positive economic development a government has greater revenue and uses the surplus for combating poverty, for example by providing such public goods as education and health services. Also in these cases, however, growth is not a compelling precondition. Even without growth greater government revenue can be achieved for example by more efficient tax collection. And leeway for social welfare spending can be gained by redistributing the budget, such as by cutting military appropriations. Furthermore, an automatic process is not given because the government can also use surplus funds for non-social purposes.

Creation of jobs due to increased economic activity can be another indirect link between economic growth and income poverty, if such a development generates income and reduces poverty. But also in this case I see no compelling causality because, for instance, industrial jobs are not necessarily open to the really poor. In addition, these positive impacts occur to a considerable extent only in the event of labour-intensive development. In many countries, however, economic growth is achieved by capital-intensive production.

Inequality, Growth and Income Poverty

If national incomes, grow, a naïve observer might assume that the income of the poor must also grow along with it. But that would be a statistical fallacy. Even if only the income of the rich grows, this results in macroeconomics statistics showing a higher per capita income. What the true conditions are, is shown as soon as one divides the population statistically into income groups, such as in fifths, as is usual. It then turns out that the bald figures on average per capita growth can certainly cloak a situation where the income of the richest fifth of the population is growing fast while that of the poorest fifth is stagnating. Despite growth, the gap between the two becomes even wider.

The unequal distribution of income (and of other assets such as property and access to social services), and its connection to poverty reduction and growth has recently returned to the forefront of the debate.

It is obvious that inequality and its changes have direct effects on the poverty situation. Does inequality also have an impact on poverty via its relation to growth, because growth promotes or reduces inequality? Earlier, the predominant view was that rapid growth was linked with at least a temporary increase in inequality, so that a distinct policy of growth initially disadvantaged the poor.

The current dominant view is that growth has no foreseeable effects on inequality and that inequality changes only very slowly, in reverse, however, it is assumed that greater equality is a determinant of growth. According to that view, an indirect relationship between poverty on one side and inequality as a factor dependent upon growth on the other is not given.

That leads to the conclusion that fair distribution has more weight than growth. Fair distribution, however, does not depend upon growth. An appropriate policy is possible at any time, not only after an economic situation has improved. The notion that still shimmers through the debate that "something must be earned first before it can be distributed", is wrong. It is a matter of designing policy and the entire economic process right from the start in such a way that the surplus benefits all including the poor. Important elements of such a policy are, for example, land reform and development of finance systems.

Relationship of Growth to Poverty

According to today's conventional wisdom, income poverty expresses only a part of what poverty means. Not least through the voices of the poor themselves, it has become clear that violation of human dignity and rights, a lack of participation in decisions and exclusion from society, unequal treatment of men and women, and vulnerability are also regarded as poverty. For poverty is caused to a great degree by conflicts of power and interests. Income poverty often is not even seen as the greatest problem.

What relationship do these more far reaching characteristics of poverty have to economic growth? A direct relationship of growth to socially-related aspects such as women's inheritance rights, land rights and exclusion from decisions cannot be seen. Considerable improvements in favour of the poor can be achieved here even without economic growth.

Those who see a strong and causal connection between economic growth and poverty reduction must ask themselves what the prospects are for high growth rates and thus for decline in poverty. Coupling poverty reduction to economic growth is problematic. If only low growth rates are to be expected.

Another question is whether continuous increases in growth are at all desirable and possible in the medium to long term. In this connection, a difference should perhaps be made between developing countries and industrialised nations. But environmental compatibility and availability of resources set limits to growth for both. Some academics assume that industrialised nations have already reached an inherent limit (stagnation theory) and that the high growth rates of earlier years will not return. Moreover, they add, full employment is no longer achievable due to, among other things, an ongoing increase in productivity, and current unemployment cannot be reduced by customary means. In any case, if growth were to be taken as the major benchmark, the prospects for a radical reduction of income poverty around the world would be modest.

Summing Up

Poverty is a complex problem and reducing it depends upon many interconnected factors that is why poverty cannot be attributed to one main cause nor its reduction based on one main strategy. Economic growth is just one strategic element among many others related to poverty reduction. An indirect causal connection between growth and poverty reduction can only be seen because governments will have a grater scope for action due to economic growth, and if they promote labour-intensive development.

Therefore growth's role in poverty reduction must be put into perspective growth cannot be the first thing that comes to mind, nor is it the golden path to reducing poverty. The simplistic theory of economic growth as the main condition obstructs the bigger picture; it clings to the underlying and ongoing belief in the trickle-down effect. Even if there is no growth or for inherent reasons there can be none, there are promising ways to take on the challenge of mass poverty in the developing countries. Up front, governments and bilateral and multilateral donors must have the political will to design economic, financial and social policies so that they are oriented on poverty in a coherent way—the result can also be economic growth.

26

Private Education

The Poor's Best Chance?

Across the developing world, private schools and education companies are not only flourishing, but reaching the poor. India is a case in point. A common assumption about the private sector in education is that it caters only to the elite, and that its promotion only serves to exacerbate inequality. On the contrary recent research points in the opposite direction. If we want to help some of the most disadvantages groups in society, then encouraging deeper private sector involvements is likely to be the best way forward.

Several developments are underway in India, all of which involve the private education sector meeting the needs of the poor in distinct ways. But India is not unique in this respect—similar phenomena are happening all over the developing world.

As a point of departure, how do government schools serve the poor? Usefully, the government sponsored Public Report on Basic Education in India (PROBE) from 1999 paints a very bleak picture of the "malfunctioning" of government schools for the poor. When researchers called unannounced on their random sample of schools, only 53 per cent had any "teaching activity' going on. In 33 per cent, the head teacher was absent. Alarmingly, the team noted that the deterioration of teaching standards was not to do with disempowered teachers, but instead could be ascribed to "plain negligence." They noted "several cases of irresponsible teachers keeping a school closed....for months at a time," many cases of drunk teachers, and head teachers who asked children to do domestic chores. Significantly, the low level of teaching activity occurred even in those schools with relative good infrastructure, teaching aids and pupil-teacher ratios.

But is there any alternative to these schools? Surely no-one else can do better than government given the resources available? As it happens, the PROBE report were serving the poor and conceded—rather reluctantly—such problems were not found in these schools. In the great majority of private schools—again visited unannounced and at random—there" was feverish classroom activity." Most parents would prefer to send their children to private schools if they could afford them. Private schools, they said, were successful because they were more accountable: "the teachers are accountable to the manager (who can fire them), and, through him or her, to the parents (who can withdraw their children)." Such accountability was not present in the government schools, and "this contrast is perceived with crystal clarity by the vast majority of parents".

The Way Forward: Loosen Regulations and Set up Voucher Schemes

To many readers, the existence of these private schools for the poor will come as a surprise. It was to me too, until I had the privilege of conducting field work for the International Finance Corporation (the private finance arm of the World Bank) on a group of such schools operating under the banner of the Federation of Private Schools" management based in Hyderabad, the federation has 500 private schools (from kindergarten to grade ten) serving poor communities in slums and villages. I was impressed by both the entrepreneurial spirit within these schools—they were run on commercial principles, not dependent on hand-outs from state or philanthropy—but also by the spirit of dedication within the schools for the poor communities served: not for nothing were the leaders of the schools known as "social workers". But these schools suffer under restrictive and inappropriate regulations. One example will suffice: to be recognised a school must deposit upto 50,000 rupees (about $1.200) in a stipulated bank account, of which neither the capital nor the interest can be touched. Given that the fees charged in these schools ranged from 25 (60 cents) to Rs. 150 per month (about $3.50) with most of the schools grouped near the lower end of the range, such sums are completely prohibitive.

Fees of around $10 per year are not affordable by everyone, but they are to a large number of poor families. Furthermore, the great majority of the schools offer a significant number of free places—up to 20 per cent—for the poorest students, allocated on the basis of claims of need checked informally in the community.

All of this suggests that if one is interested in serving the needs of the poor in India, then trying to reform the totally inadequate, cumbersome and unaccountable government system is unlikely to be the best way. Instead, reform the regulatory environment to make it suitable for the flourishing of private schools for the poor, help build private financing schemes using overseas and indigenous philanthropy, and encourage public voucher schemes so that parents can use their allowance of funding where they see the schools are performing well, rather than wasting them in unresponsive state schools.

Private education in developing countries isn't just about the poor, of course, and there are many exciting examples of big education businesses. But these too have implications for the ways in which the private sector can reach the least advantaged. One Indian company which embodies much of the excite the National Institute for Information Technology (NIIT). With its competitor, Aptech, it shares just over 70 per cent of the information technology education and training market in India estimated at roughly Rs. 1.1 billion ($24 million). NIIT has 40 wholly owned centres in the metropolitan areas, and about 1,000 franchised centres across India. It also has a global reach, with centres in the U.S. Asian Pacific, Europe, Japan, Central Asia and Africa. A key aspect of NIIT's educational philosophy is that there is a need to harness research to improve the efficiency of learning and to raise educational standards.

Because of its success in developing innovative and cost-effective IT education and training, NIIT has attracted the attention of several state governments. First off the mark was Tamil Nadu, which wanted to bring a computer curriculum to all of its high schools. Significantly, although allocating about $22 million over five years to this endeavour, it didn't hand the funds over to government schools, perhaps in light of the PROBE report's lessons. Instead, it developed a model to contract out the service to private companies, which provide the software and hardware, while the government supplies electricity and the class room. For the first round of the Tamil Nadu process, 43 contracts were awarded for 666 schools, with NIIT allotted 371 schools. Many of the classrooms have become NIIT centre, open to school children and teachers I daytime, then used by the franchise holder in the evenings. The contracting out of curriculum areas such as this represents an important step forward in relationships between the public and private sectors, and provides an interesting model worth watching and emulating.

Most recently, NIIT has focused on reaching largely illiterate and unschooled children through the Internet. Within weeks of having set up an "Internet kiosk" in a slum area, the institute's researchers found that without any instruction, children could achieve a remarkable level of computer literacy. NIIT is exploring ways to roll out the idea commercially, harnessing the power of the private sector to reach the poorest through modern technology.

These initiatives all find echoes in other developing countries. In each case, the private, not the public sector, is most responsive to the needs of the poor, and is brining innovation, efficiency and educational quality to the lives of the most disadvantaged. The private sector has the potential to promote greater equity and to influence education policy, provided it is encouraged and viewed as a partner, not a threat to governments, whether in the developing or the developed world.

could bring about drastic changes in the location of the world's agro-ecological zones. Farmers will require new crop varieties capable of producing under diverse conditions, without adding ever-increasing amounts of fertilizers and other agro-chemicals. Because of the limited scope for growth in the world's cultivated areas, each new generation of varieties will have to be more productive than its predecessors.

Much has been written about the use of genetic engineering in plant breeding. Modern molecular techniques can be used to transfer genes from one living organism to another or to change the genetic material within to produce more desirable traits. Genetic Engineering has enormous potential to help solve problems that have proved intractable using conventional breeding approaches, such as developing crop varieties with in-built resistance to keep pests and diseases and tolerance to stresses such as drought. However, the possible impact of these techniques, particularly on human health and the environment, is giving rise to fierce worldwide debate.

Take the case of banana and its close relative plantain, two of the developing world's most important crops. Their improvement is hindered by the sterility of most cultivars, a problem that can be addressed through genetic engineering. It is now possible to transfer gene constructs, such as those associated with disease resistance, directly into varieties with other desirable characteristics, drastically reducing the need for pesticides.

Today, research on genetic engineering is focussed on the development of commercial varieties of the world's major crops of interest to industrialised farmers. Many of the staple crops of importance to poor farmers in developing countries, such as cassava, bananas, beans and yams, have received relatively little attention. This situation is likely to continue as plant breeding is increasingly privatised and biotechnology becomes the fast-growing province of private industry. Meanwhile, the high costs of the new technologies are quickly exceeding the capacity of many, if not most, public research institutions—both in developing and developed countries—to support them. Thus, for the time being, increasing agriculture's role in the development of the world's poor is likely to continue to depend on the identification, maintenance and use of genetic diversity.

28

Sex and Gender

A World of Difference

Understanding the differences between women and men, and how they are determined, is of key importance in understanding why a gender perspective is so important for development and the elimination of world poverty.

Differences between women and men are determined by biology, on the one hand, and society, on the other.

- Sex marks the distinction between women and men as result of the fundamental biological, physical and genetic difference between them.

- Gender roles are set by convention and other social, economic, political and cultural forces.

The precise boundary between these factors is the subject of fierce debate. Some people believe that the only important difference is that women can bear children and men cannot. Others believe that biology determines a much wider set of characteristics, attributes and capabilities. Whatever the case, the wide variation in the position of women in different societies around the world demonstrates that, unlike sex, gender roles are by no means fixed by nature—they are made by people, and can be renegotiated and changed.

The position of women in society is far from being of academic interest alone. It not only has fundamental consequences for the quality of life of both women and men, but also has a direct impact on a society's prosperity and well-being. The government's policy on international development recognises that gender-based inequality is a major obstacle to the escape from poverty. Studies have shown that developing countries which strive to ensure that women have equal rights have higher rates of economic growth, lower mortality rates, smaller and healthier families, and a better-educated population. Changing gender roles can make a world of difference.

The evidence also shows that gender equality is not luxury which can only be afforded by rich countries. UN data reveals that some developing countries outperform much richer ones in the opportunities they afford women. The better performing countries are scattered throughout the world showing that culture and religion need not be barriers to the advancement of women.

The gender gap in many countries is closing fast. Rapid progress has been made in recent decades. But in no society do women fare as well as men. Women are gaining ground in health and education terms, but still have a long way to go in sharing political and economic opportunities. They continue to suffer high levels of violence and abuse, and in many countries are treated differently to men by the law. These disadvantages are not due to sex differences, but are the result of gender discrimination.

Empowerment, Equality and Equity: What do they Mean?

Women's empowerment, gender equality and equity are key terms in debates about the changes required in the relationships between women and men.

- ***Empowerment*** means individuals acquiring the power to think and act freely, exercise choice, and to fulfil their potential as full and equal members of society.
- ***Equality*** means that women should have the same rights and entitlements as men to human, social,

economic and cultural development, and equal voice in civil and political life. It does not mean that everyone should be the same, or that the benefits of development should be shared in exactly equal proportions by everyone. This would be neither feasible nor desirable, and would not be consistent with the notion of empowerment, which upholds everyone's right to determine their own future and the lifestyle of their choice.

- ***Equity*** means that the exercise of these rights should lead to outcomes which are fair and just, and which enable women to have the same power as men to define and pursue the objectives of development and shape societies of the future.

The difference between equality and equity is important because it underlines the rights of women to define the objectives of development for themselves and to seek outcomes which are not necessarily identical to those sought or enjoyed by men. Women have the right to pursue development paths which reflect their own needs and aspirations.

Upholding these rights is in the interests of men as well as women, because of the wider social and economic benefits brought by gender equality. Because of the universal disadvantages experienced by women, their empowerment is crucial to the achievement of equality and equity, the elimination of poverty and a better world for all.

29

Democracy and Poverty

Are they Interlinked?

Democracy assistance and poverty reduction are rightly becoming two focal and related—issues for development assistance. Increasingly, many organisations, including intergovernmental, national and civil society, are focusing their work on these two areas. Futhermore, the relationship between these two issues is complex and ever changing. There is thus a need to develop methodologies of linking democracy assistance and poverty reduction at both the policy and programme levels. International IDEA (Institute for Democracy and Electoral Assistance) in cooperation with the World Bank and the United Nations Development Programme, is developing concrete strategies that address these two objectives in a mutually reinforcing way. Through an overall situation analysis followed by regional meetings in sub-Saharan Africa, South Asia, Latin America, the Caucasus and the Arab region, the Institute has marshalled evidence of some of the key problems that affect democracy consolidation and poverty reduction in these countries:

- Corruption and its undermining effect on popular confidence in public institutions.
- Continuing economic instability coupled with the lack of strategies for addressing the twin challenges of poverty and increasing popular participation in its alleviation.

- The extremely limited nature of citizen's influence on overall policy and decision-making processes despite the spread of formal democratic institutions.
- A trend in many post-communist states towards viewing growing poverty as a direct consequence of a transition to democracy.

In short, the evidence is not very encouraging for the prospects for democracy consolidation and poverty reduction. The critical step, International IDEA, advocates is the development of an approach that not only seeks to put democracy assistance and poverty reduction on top of the development assistance agenda, but also to encourage all involved to treat them as twin elements of an integrated programme of action.

Through a focus on accountable governance, promotion and protection of citizenship and rights and increased popular participation, International IDEA believes that both democracy and poverty reduction can be addressed simultaneously. Policy recommendations are being developed and will be shared in the course of this year with governments, international organisations and civil society bodies.

International IDEA believes that democracy promotion can be used as a tool for fulfilling a variety of objectives. Democracy matters because it protects human right and preserves human dignity. But democracy also matters because it helps to address some of the most critical challenges facing states today: peace, development, economic growth and stability.

Democracy does not guarantee any one of these, but increasingly it seems to be a precondition for them in the long term. Thus, advocating democracy goes beyond being a moral issue; it becomes *fundamental* to advancing the well-being of people and the stability of states. International IDEA will continue to explore the link between democracy and the major issues facing society today—and continue to argue the case for democracy.

30

Will Education Go to Market?

The World Trade Organisation has launched processes that could open up to competition the expanding and highly protected world market in education. What issues are at stake? Mot of us see education as first and foremost a public service which is responsible for providing young people with instruction. For investors looking for somewhere to put their money it is also an annual budget of $1,000 billion worldwide, a sector employing 50 million people, and above all a billion potential customers in the form of students.

The decision to extend services the liberalisation of international trade which previously applied to commodities was taken in 1994. The General Agreement on Trade in Services (GATS) which was signed in April of that year included education on the list of services to be liberalised. To say outside the scope of this agreement a country's education system must be completely financed and administered by the state, which is no longer the case anywhere. However, each country can still decide freely what commitments it wants to make, and especially which educational sectors it wants to expose to market forces. The New Zealand government, for example, has decided to open up to outside competition the whole private education sector, from primary to university level.

So far, New Zealand is an exception, but that situation is likely to change. Part 4 of the GATS agreement ("Progressive liberalisation") requires that fresh negotiations should be held by the end of 2000 at the latest, and should be directed to "the elimination of the adverse effects on trade in services of measures as a means of providing effective market access". At the Geneva headquarters of the World Trade Organisation (WTO), far from the headlines and the demonstrators, work still goes on. But independently of the WTO and national policies, a number of factors are driving educational systems towards "communication".

Pressures for Change

First, education is a rapidly-growing sector in which governments are finding it harder and harder to satisfy demand, above all in higher education. Between 1985 and 1992, the number of students in higher education rose about 26 per cent—from 58.6 to 73.7 million. Meanwhile, public spending on education has tended to stagnate over the past 15 years (5-6 per cent of GDP in rich countries and 4 per cent elsewhere).

In view of this dearth of public spending, parents and students are increasingly looking to private education for a solution. In the United States, every episode of violence in a state school and every scandal that rocks official school systems gives a boost to "home schooling", where children no longer attend school and are taught at home.

Traditional public education is also coming in for strong criticism. Employers complain it is not geared to their needs and is not flexible enough. Under pressure from economic interests, a process of "deregulating" education system has begun. The growing independence of schools is encouraging them to look for alternative sources of funding, ranging from sponsorship to full management by private companies and including many kinds of partnerships between schools and firms. The time for out-of-school education has come... the liberalisation of the educational process thereby made possible will lead to control by education service providers who are more innovative than the traditional structures.

The development and spread of information and communication technologies on a massive scale make possible the development of paid distance learning, using multimedia and the Internet for tutorials, examinations, etc.

Secondary and primary education are also affected. More and more paying Internet sites bill themselves as alternatives to state schools or traditional private schools. The computer screen takes over from the teacher, for a fee of around $2,250 a year.

The WTO secretariat set up a working group in 1998 to look at prospectus for more liberalised education. Its report pointed to the rapid growth of distance learning and noted the increasing number of partnerships between educational institutions and private firms.

Education for Export

Some 350 U.S. experts on international trade in services, including 170 businessmen and women, gathered at the U.S. Commerce Department in Washington on October 16, 1998 to draw up recommendations for the U.S. negotiators at the WTO. The purpose of the meeting, called Services 2000, was to look at how the U.S. government should continue to support the efforts of American business to take competitive advantage in foreign markets". The US currently controls about 16 per cent of the world market in services. Its services exports have more than doubled in the past 10 years and now cover 42 per cent of the non-services trade deficit.

The United States is also the world's leading exporter of educational services, and a working group at the Services 2000 conference paid special attention to this sector. It concluded that the sector "needs the same degree of transparency, transferability and interchangeability, mutual recognition, and freedom from undue regulation or restraints and barriers that the United States acknowledges on behalf of other service industries". The report said that three points should be at the centre of WTO negotiations about education.

Firstly, there should be a free flow of electronic information and means of communication, nationally and internationally. Secondly, the negotiators should tackle "barriers and other restrictions that limit or prevent the provision of educational and training services across countries and internationally." They were also to deal with obstacles to the transferability of degree and diplomas.

Fighting for Market Share

The U.S. demands are backed by most countries of the APEC (Asia-Pacific Economic Cooperation) zone. In a note in October 1999, the Australian delegation to the WTO said it would be "encouraging all members to make expanded commitments in all sectors, even the ones that have proved difficult in both regional and multilateral services negotiations", particularly education.

South Korea took a similar position. At a meeting of ministers of Human Resources from APEC Countries that it hosted in September 1997, the Seoul government put out a memorandum which clearly stated its vision of education as a tool of economic competition.

"The emphasis on education for itself or on education for good members of a community without a large emphasis on preparation for future work is no longer appropriate. Such a view of education and work cannot be justified in a world where economic development is emphasised.

"At present, in many economies, the education system do not sufficiently reflect labour market conditions. Their inflexible and inefficient education systems could not meet the new economic environmental challenges." So education should be made more "flexible", i.e. be deregulated and liberalised. In particular, "School systems should be established to allow all students to study what they are interested in "and "employers, with school educators, should share the role of educating students".

Some think resistance to liberalizing education will come from Europe, especially France. "The future WTO negotiations cannot call in question France's tradition of public service in the field of education and health", stressed a report on the WTO.

Bibliography

Books

A.C. Pigou (1960). *The Economics of Welfare,* Macmillan & Co. Ltd., London.

Ahluwalia, Montek, S. (1985). "Rural Poverty, Agricultural Production and Prices: A Re-Examination" in John Mellor and Desai Gunvant, M. (eds.) *Agricultural Changes and Rural Poverty,* The John Hopkins University Press, London.

Amartya Sen (1995). *The Hindu,* 6th November, Interviewed by Ramamanohar Reddy, Chennai.

Betellei, A. (2000). *Chronicles of Over Time,* Penguine Books, New Delhi.

Carr, Maryn *et al.,* (1997). *Speaking out; Women's Economic Empowerment in South Asia,* Vikas Publications, New Delhi.

Chakravarty, Sukhamoy (1989), *Development Planning, The Indian Experience,* Oxford University Press, New Delhi.

Charsely, S.R. and G.K. Karnath (1998). *Challenging Untouchability. Dalit Initiative and Experience from Karnataka,* Sage Publications, New Delhi.

Chinnadurai, K. (1986). *Evaluation Study of Implementation of IRDP,* State Bank of India, Coimbatore.

Dantwala, M.L. (1996). *Dilemmas of Growth: The Indian Experience,* Sagar Publications, New Delhi.

Delige, R. (1999). *The Untouchables of India,* Berg, New York.

Desai, B.M. and N.V. Namboodiri (1993). *Rural Financial Institutions: Promotion and Performance,* Oxford and IBH Publishing Company Pvt. Ltd., New Delhi.

Dev, S. Mahendra (1999), "State Interventions and Women's Employment", in T.S. Papola and Alakh N. Sharma (Eds.). *Gender and Employment in India;* Vikas Publishing House Pvt. Ltd., New Delhi, pp. 373-411.

Dharm Narain & Sen, A.K. *et al.* (1989), *Studies on Indian Agriculture,* Oxford University Press, New Delhi.

Frencine Fournier (1997), *Foreword, Poverty and Participation in Civil Society.* Edited by Yogesh Atal of Else Oyen, Abhinav Publications, New Delhi.

George Psacharopoulos and Moureen Woodhall (1986). *Education for Development: An Analysis of Investment Choices,* Oxford, New York.

Griffin (1979). *The Political Economy of Agrarian Change,* The Macmillan Press Ltd., London.

Griffin Keith (1978), *International Inequality and National Poverty.* The Macmillan Press Ltd., London.

Griffin Keith (1981). *Land Concentration and Rural Poverty,* The Macmillan Press Ltd., Hong Kong.

Gunnar Myrdal (1968). *Asian Drama—An Inquiry into Poverty of Nations,* Pantheon, New York.

Gunnar Myrdal (1970). *The Challenge of World Poverty: A World Anti-Poverty Programme in Outline,* Pantheon, New York.

Gupta, D. (2000). *Interrogating Caste: Understanding Hierarchy and Difference in Indian Society,* Penguine Books, New Delhi.

Haq, Mahabub Ul (1978). *The Poverty Curtain: Choices for the Third World,* Oxford University Press, Bombay.

Haq, Mahabub Ul (1997). *Human Development in South Asia,* Oxford University Press, New York.

Harper, M. (1998). "*Profit for the Poor*", Oxford and IBH Publishing Co., Delhi.

Hirway Indira (1984). *Programmes for Poverty Eradication: A Critique of Target Group Approach,* Sardar Patel Institute for Economic and Social Research (Mimeo).

Holcombe, Susan (1995). *Managing to Empower: The Grameena Bank's Experience of Poverty Alleviation,* Oxford University Press, Dhaka.

IFMR (1984). *An Economic Assessment of Poverty Eradication and Rural Unemployment Alleviation Programme and their Prospects,* Madras.

Jackson Dudley (1972). *Poverty, MacMillan Studies in Economics,* MacMillan, London.

Karmakar, K.G. (1999). *Rural Credit and Self-Help Groups, Micro-Finance Needs and Concepts in India.* Sage Publications, New Delhi.

Kaushik Dasu (1984). *The Development Economy: A Critique of Contemporary Theory.* Oxford University Press, Delhi.

Khan Azizur Rahman & Eddy Lee (1984). *Poverty in Rural Asia,* Asian Employment Programme (ARTEP), Inernational Labour Organisation, Bangkok, Thailand.

Kuznets S. (1965). *Economic Growth and Structure,* Heinemann, London.

Lewis, A. (1966). *Development Planning,* Allen & Unwin, London.

Mahammad Haan Khan (1981). *Underdevelopment and Agrarian Structure in Pakistan,* A West View Replica Edition, West View Press, U.S.A.

Maheswari, S.R. (1985), *Rural Development in India,* Sage Publications, Delhi.

Minhas, R.S. (1974). *Planning and the Poor,* S. Chand & Company Limited, New Delhi.

Mukta Mittal (1995). *Women Power in India,* Anmol Publications Pvt. Ltd., New Delhi.

Myrdal Gunner (1968). *Asian Drama, Volume III,* Twentieth Century Fund, New York.

NABARD (1999). *Banking with the Poor: Financing Self-Help Groups,* CGM, NABARD, Hyderabad.

NABARD (1999-2000), *NABARD and Micro-Finance,* Mumbai.

Nanda, Y.C. (2000). *Role of Banks in Rural Development in the New Millennium,* National Bank for Agriculture and Rural Development, Mumbai.

NCERT (2000). *Human Development in South India,* Oxford, New Delhi.

Parthasarathy, G. (1982). "Integrated Rural Development Concepts, Theoretical Base and Contradiction, in *"Development Planning and Policy",* Edited by Gupta D.B., *et al.,* Wiley Eastern, New Delhi.

Rahman, Hossain Zillus (1998). *Poverty Issues in Bangladesh,* Power and Participation Research Centre, Mimeo.

Rai & Tandon (1999). *Voluntary Development Organisation and Socio-Economic Development,* Indian Economic Association, 82nd Conference Volume, Amritsar.

Sakuntala Narasimhan (1999). *Empowering Women, An Alternative for Strategy from Rural India,* Sage Publications, New Delhi.

Sen A.K. (1984). Poverty and Famines: *An Essay on Entitlement and Deprivation,* Oxford University Press, Delhi.

Shylendra, H.S. (1999), *Promoting Women's Self-Help Groups: Lessons from an Action Research Project of IRMA,* Anand, India, Working Paper No. 121.

The World Bank (2000-2001). *World Development Report,* Oxford, New York.

Todaro Michael, P. (1977). *Economics for a Developing World,* Longmans, London.

Todaro Michael, P. (1990). *Economics for a Developing World,* Second Edition, Longmans, New York.

Von Braun, J., Bayes, F. and Akhter, R. (1999). *Village Pay Phones and Poverty Reduction.* ZEF Discussion Papers on Development Policy No. 18, Centre for Development Research, University of Berlin.

Von Pischke, J.D. *et al.,* (1983). *Rural Financial Markets in Developing Countries: Their Use and Abuse,* John Hopkins University, Baltimore, U.S.A.

Yogesh Atal (1996). *Poverty and Participation of Civil Society,* Abhinav Publications, New Delhi.

Zeller, Manfred and Manohar Sharma (1998). *Rural Finance and Poverty Alleviation,* Food Policy Report, International Food Policy Research Institute, Washington DC, USA.

Journals

Amitava Mukherjee (1999). *Out of the Abysis. The Challenge Confronting Some Civil Society Actors,* Indian Economic Association, 82 Conference, Amritsar.

Awasthi, P.K., *et al.,* (1986). 'IRDP: Receptivity and Reaction', *Indian Journal of Agricultural Economics,* Vol. 41, No. 4, October-December.

Bagchee, Sandeep (1987). 'Poverty Alleviation Programmes in Seventh Plan: An Appraisal', *Economic and Political Weekly,* Vol. XXII, No. 4, January 24.

Bardhan, P.K. (1973). 'On the Incidence of Poverty in Rural India of the Sixties, *Economic and Political Weekly,* Februry.

Bhat, Mazi, P.N., *et al.,* (1999). Finding of National Family Health Survey Regional Analysis, *Economic and Political Weekly.* Vol. XXXIV, Nos. 42 and 43. Oct. 16-22/23-29.

Chambers, Robert (1994). *"Poverty and Livelihoods Whose Reality Counts?" Overview Paper II, UNDP Stockholm Roundtable,* "Change: Social Conflict or Harmony?" 22-24 July.

Copertake, James G. (1996). *The Resilience of IRDP: Reform and Perpetuation of an Indian Myth, Development Policy Review,* 14.

Dantwala, M.L. (1983). "Rural Development: Investment Without Organisation', *Economic and Political Weekly.*

Desai, A.R. (1987). 'Rural Development and Human Rights in Independent India, *Economic and Political Weekly,* Vol. XXII, No. 31.

Desai, B.M. and J.W. Mellor (1993). "Institutional Finance for Agricultural Development: An Analytical Survey of Critical Issues", *Food Policy Review I, International Food Policy Research Institute, Washington, DC, USA.*

Ghosh, D.K. (1995), Group Cohesiveness in DWCRA Groups: An Application of Sociometric Approach, *Kurukshetra*, May-June.

Govil, R.K. (1982). 'Micro-Level Planning and Rural Development', *Kurukshetra.*

Grewal, R.S. et al., (1985). 'Impact of Integrated Rural Development Programme on Rural Women in Bhiwani District of Haryana', *Indian Journal of Agricultural Economics,* Vol. XL, No. 3, July-September.

Hara Gopal, G. & Balaramulu, Ch. 'Poverty Alleviation Programmes: IRDP in an Andhra Pradesh District, *Economic and Political Weekly,* Vol. XXIV, Nos. 35 & 36, September 2-9.

Hirway Indira (1984). *Programmes for Poverty Eradication: A Critique of Target Group Approach,* Sardar Patel Institute for Economic and Social Research (Mimeo).

Jain, S.C. (1986). 'Poverty Alleviation Programmes in India: Some Issues of Micro Policy', *Indian Journal of Agricultural Economics,* Vol. XLI, No. 3, Conference Number, July-September.

Karmakar, K.G. (1999). *Rural Credit and Self-Help Groups: Micro-Finance Needs and Concepts in India,* Sage Publications, New Delhi.

Kumar Rajinder, *et al.,* (1986). 'Impact of Credit on Income, Employment and Capital Formulation of Rural Poor', *Indian Journal of Agricultural Economics,* Vol. 41, No. 4, October-December.

M.S. Kallur (2001). 'Empowerment of Women Through NGOs: A Case Study of MYRADA Self-Help Groups', Indian Journal of Agricultural Economics, Vol. 56, No. 3.

Mosley, P. and R.P. Dahal (1985). "Lending to the Poorest: Early Lessons from the Small Farmers: Development Programme, Nepal", Development Policy Review, Vol. 3, No. 2.

NIRD (1985), 'Employment and Income Generation Through IRDP, NREP and DRM', *Journal of Rural Development,* Vol. 4, No. 5, March-September.

Owusu, K. Opoku and William Tetteh (1982). "An Experiment in Agricultural Credit: The Small Farmer Group Lending Programme in Ghana", *Savings and Development,* Vol. I, No. 1.

Rajaram Das Gupta (2001). "Working and Impact of Rural Self-Help Groups and other forms of Micro Financing", *Indian Journal of Agricultural Economics,* Vol. 56, No. 3.

Rajasekhar, D., (1996), "Problems and Prospects of Group Lending in NGO Credit Programme in India", Savings and Development, Vol. 20, No. 1.

Sinha, S.P. & Prasad Jagadish (1980). 'Special Programmes for Weaker Sections: An Evaluation', *Indian Journal of Agricultural Economics,* Vol. XXXV, No. 4.

Stiglitz, J.E. (1990), "Paper Monitoring and Credit Markets", *The World Bank Economic Review,* Vol. 4, No. 3.

Thakur, D.S. (1977). 'Rural Development in India: Past Experience and Tasks Ahead', *Indian Journal of Agricultural Economics,* Vol. XXXII, No. 3, July-September.

The Hindu, 11th May 2002, Chennai.

Yaron, J. (1992). *Successful Rural Finance Institutions,* World Bank Discussion Paper, 150, Washington, DC, USA.

Reports

Amitava Mukherjee (1999), *Out of the Abysis. The Challenge Confronting Some Civil Society Actors,* Indian Economic Association, 82 Conference, Amritsar.

APDPIP (2000), *On Andhra Pradesh District Poverty Initiatives Project Appraisal Document (PAD), Report No. 20089,* South Asia Regional Office.

Chief Planning Officer (2001). *Hand Book of Statistics, Mahabubnagar District,* Mahabubnagar.

Chief Planning Officer Collectorate (2000). *Hand Book of Statistics, Krishna District,* Machilipatnam.

Chief Planning Officer Collectorate (2001). *Hand Book of Statics, Chittoor District,* Chittoor.

CIRDAP (1998). *Increased Household Income and Rural Women in Asia, Impact on Status and Activities,* Dhaka, Bangladesh.

CIRDAP (1998). *Poverty Gender and Participation,* Dhaka.

CIRDAP (1999), *Rural Development Report, Centre on Integrated Rural Development for Asia and Pacific,* Dhaka.

CIRDAP (2000). *Poverty Gender and Participation,* Dhaka.

CMIE (2000). *Profile of Districts, Economic Intelligence Service,* October, Mumbai.

Government of Andhra Pradesh (1998). *Annual Report of the Commission of the Rural Development,* Hyderabad.

Government of Andhra Pradesh (1999). *Annual Report of the Commission of the Rural Development,* Hyderabad.

Government of Andhra Pradesh (1999). *New Series on State Domestic Product,* A.P., Hyderabad.

Government of Andhra Pradesh (2001). *Provisional Population Totals, Series 29,* Hyderabad.

Government of Andhra Pradesh (2001) *Statistical Abstract,* Hyderabad.

Government of Andhra Pradesh (2001). *Strategy Paper,* Hyderabad.

Government of India (1991). *Census of India,* New Delhi.

Government of India (1997-2002). *IX Five Year Plan,* New Delhi.

Government of India (2001). *Provisional Population Totals,* New Delhi.

Government of India (1974). *Towards Equality—Committee on the Status of Women in India.*

Government of India (1998, 99). *Reports of the Commissioner of SC and STs,* New Delhi.

Haq, Mahbub Ul. (1997). *Human Development in South Asia*, Oxford University Press, New York.

Holcombe, Susan (1995). *Managing to Empower. The Grameen Banks' Experience of Poverty Alleviation*, Oxford University Press, Dhaka.

IFAD (1996). *The State of World Poverty, Rome for a Discussion on the Process and Structural Causes of Poverty,* see Rovert Chambers (1983). Rural Development, Putting the last First, London, Longmans, one of the best discussions on how these perpetuate poverty.

IFAD (2001). *Rural Poverty Report, The Challenge of Ending Rural Poverty,* Oxford, New York.

Indian Bank (2002-2003). *Annual Credit Plan, Krishna District (A.P.),* Vijayawada.

International Fund for Agricultural Development (IFAD) (1992). *The State World Rural Poverty—An Inquiry into its Causes and Consequences,* New York University Press, New York.

ISACPA (1992). *Independent South Asia Commission or Poverty Alleviation.*

NABARD (1999). *Annual Report, Mumbai.*

NABARD (2000): *Annual Report,* Mumbai.

NABARD (2001): *Annual Report,* Mumbai.

NIRD (1994). *Rural Development Report: Rural Employment,* Hyderabad, Andhra Pradesh.

NIRD (2001). *National Conference on SHG Movement in the Country & Swarnajayanti Gram Swarozgar Yojana (SGSY).* National Institute of Rural Development, Hyderabad.

PEO (1985). *Evaluation Report on Integrated Rural Development Programme,* New Delhi.

RBI (1984). *Implementation of Integrated Rural Development Programme*—A Field Study.

SAARC (1992). *The Independent Source Asian Commissions of the SAARC on Poverty Alleviation,* Dhaka.

South Asian Association for Regional Co-operation (SAARC) (1992). *Meeting the Challenge, Report of the Independent South Asian Commission on Poverty.*

The World Bank (1990). *World Development Report,* Oxford, New York.

The World Bank (1991). *Gender and Poverty in India,* Washington DC.

The World Bank (1999-2000). *World Development Report 1999-2000,* Oxford University Press, New Delhi.

UNDP (1994). *Human Development Report,* Oxford, New York.

UNDP (1996). *Human Development Report,* Oxford, New York.

UNDP (1997). *Human Development Report,* Oxford, New York.

UNDP (2000). *Human Development Report,* Oxford, New York.

World Bank (1990). *World Development Report—Poverty,* Oxford University Press.

Yerramaraju, B. and Firdausi, A.A. (1995). *Evaluation of DWCRA in Prakasam District.* Sponsored by Government of Andhra Pradesh. Administrative Staff College of India, Hyderabad.

Others

Government of Andhra Pradesh, *Vision-2020,* Hyderabad.

Government of India (1985). *Five Year Plan Documents (The Seventh and Eighth Five Year Plans 1985-95),* New Delhi, The Planning Commission.

NABARD (1984). *Study of Implementation of IRDP (Mimeo),* Bombay.

Government of Andhra Pradesh (1999). *Vision-2020,* Hyderabad, India.

Government of Andhra Pradesh, *Guidelines for Swarnajayanti Gram Swarozgar Yojana, Panchayati Raj and Rural Development Department,* Hyderabad.

IXth Five Year Plan (1997-2000).

The Hindu (2002). April 27, Chennai.

The Hindu, Vision 2020.

Index